# DATE DUE

| | | | |
|---|---|---|---|
| NV 6 95 | | | |
| DE 16 99 | | | |
| | | | |
| | | | |
| | | | |
| | | | |
| | | | |
| | | | |
| | | | |
| | | | |
| | | | |
| | | | |
| | | | |
| | | | |
| | | | |
| | | | |
| | | | |
| | | | |

DEMCO 38-296

PRESENTING

# Ursula K. Le Guin

Twayne's United States Authors Series
Young Adult Authors

Patricia J. Campbell, General Editor

TUSAS 677

Ursula K. Le Guin
*Courtesy of Lisa Kroeber.*

# PRESENTING

# Ursula K. Le Guin

## Suzanne Elizabeth Reid

*Emory & Henry College*

Twayne Publishers
An Imprint of Simon & Schuster Macmillan
New York

Prentice Hall International
London  Mexico City  New Delhi  Singapore  Sydney  Toronto

*Presenting Ursula K. Le Guin*
Suzanne Elizabeth Reid

Copyright © 1997 by Twayne Publishers

Twayne Publishers
An Imprint of Simon & Schuster Macmillan
1633 Broadway
New York, NY 10019

**Library of Congress Cataloging-in-Publication Data**

Reid, Suzanne Elizabeth.
    Presenting Ursula Le Guin / Suzanne Elizabeth Reid.
        p.    cm. — (Twayne's United States authors series ; TUSAS
677. Young adult authors)
    Includes bibliographical references and index.
    Summary: A critical introduction to the life and work of the
science fiction novelist Ursula K. Le Guin.
    ISBN 0-8057-4609-9 (alk. paper)
    1. Le Guin, Ursula K., 1929–    —Criticism and interpretation.
2. Young adult fiction, American—History and criticism.    3. Women
and literature—United States—History, 20th century.    4. Science
fiction, American—History and criticism.    [1. Le Guin, Ursula K.,
1929–    —Criticism and interpretation.    2. American literature—
History and criticism.    3. Science fiction—History and criticism.]
    I. Title    II. Series: Twayne's United States authors series ; TUSAS
    677.    III. Series: Twayne's United States authors series.    Young
    adult authors.
PS3562.E42Z87    1997                                         96-38622
813'.54—dc20                                                          CIP

The paper used in this publication meets the minimum requirements of
American National Standard for Information Services—Permanence of
Paper for Printed Library Materials. ANSI Z3948-1984. ∞™

10 9 8 7 6 5 4 3 2 1

Printed in the United States of America

*In honor of my father, Dr. Alexander August Schmid,
who taught me to think independently,
and in appreciation for my family—Dr. Robin Reid, Jenny,
and Tristan—who give me the security to be free.*

# Contents

# Foreword

The advent of Twayne's Young Adult Authors Series in 1985 was a response to the growing stature and value of adolescent literature and the lack of serious critical evaluation of the new genre. The first volume of the series was heralded as marking the coming-of-age of young adult fiction. The aim of the series is twofold. First, it enables young readers to research the work of their favorite authors and to see them as real people. Each volume is written in a lively, readable style and attempts to present in an attractive, accessible format a vivid portrait of the author as a person. Second, the series provides teachers and librarians with insights and background material for promoting and teaching young adult novels. Each of the biocritical studies is a serious literary analysis of one author's work (or one subgenre within young adult literature), with attention to plot structure, theme, character, setting, and imagery. In addition, many of the series writers delve deeper into the creative writing process by tracking down early drafts or unpublished manuscripts by their subject authors, consulting with their editors or other mentors, and examining influences from literature, film, or social movements. Many of the contributing authors of the series are among the leading scholars and critics of adolescent literature. Some are even young adult novelists themselves. Most of the studies are based on extensive interviews with the subject author, and each includes an exhaustive study of his or her work. Although the general format is the same, the individual volumes are uniquely shaped by their subjects, and each brings a different perspective to the classroom. The goal of the series is to produce a succinct but comprehensive study of the life and art of every leading young adult author writing in the United States today. The books trace how that art has been accepted by readers and critics, evaluate its place in the developing field of adolescent literature, and—perhaps most important—inspire a reading and rereading of this quality fiction that speaks so directly to young people about their life experiences.

PATRICIA J. CAMPBELL, GENERAL EDITOR

# Preface

I am not a scholar of Ursula K. Le Guin; I am a reader of her works who becomes frustrated with Ged's stubborn pride, who yearns to give Therru a careful hug, and who doesn't quite get Shevek's theory of simultaneity. I picked, grazed, and pondered my way through *Always Coming Home* while my family drove across the country from Southwest Virginia to San Diego and back again, in a reversal of the trip Le Guin describes in her poetic essay "Place Names" (1981). I have read, reread, and read about the works mentioned here. My life is changed.

"Don't reduce my stories to mere ideas" writes Le Guin, "They are more than that." Yes they are. They are experiences that make me, as the reader, laugh, worry, mope, and sometimes wonder "What on Earth is this all about?" Because all of her stories, although they sometimes take place elsewhere, are about what is happening on Earth to humans. Her writing makes us think, perhaps in ways we have not thought before. As a citizen and teacher who is deeply concerned about students who don't see hope for peace among people and who fear that their Earth is being irreparably destroyed, I value this ability to open minds to new ideas.

My goal for this book is not to recreate Le Guin's ideas, but to provide a framework of information and raise the kinds of questions that help readers notice and appreciate the many layers of her work. I have tried to write a helpful introduction to her work.

I would like to thank Patty Campbell for giving me the motivation to explore all of Le Guin's work and write this book. I also am grateful to Virginia Kidd for sharing photographs and to

Ursula K. Le Guin for her wonderful letters. I appreciate their trust. Especially, I want to acknowledge my husband, Robin, for his constant encouragement, and my children for their love and appreciation. Thanks.

# Chronology

**1967**   *City of Illusions* released by Ace.

**1968**   *A Wizard of Earthsea* published by Parnassus. Spends husband's sabbatical year in England.

**1969**   *The Left Hand of Darkness* is published and honored. (See Appendix for list of selected honors and awards.)

**1970**   *The Tombs of Atuan* published.

**1971**   *The Lathe of Heaven* released by Scribner's Sons.

**1972**   "The Word for World Is Forest" appears in *Again, Dangerous Visions*. *The Farthest Shore* published by Parnassus as final book of the Earthsea Trilogy.

**1973**   Receives National Book Award for *The Farthest Shore*. Publishes *From Elfland to Poughkeepsie* (essays and lectures).

**1974**   *The Dispossessed: An Ambiguous Utopia* appears.

**1975**   Publishes *The Wind's Twelve Quarters* (short stories), *Dreams Must Explain Themselves* (critical essays), and *Wild Angels* (poems). Appears as guest of honor at Aussiecon, a science fiction conference in Melbourne, Australia. Receives another Fulbright scholarship, traveling to England.

**1976**   Teaches creative writing at the University of Reading in England. *Very Far Away from Anywhere Else* and *Orsinian Tales* (short stories) appear, and *The Word for World Is Forest* is published as a novel.

**1977**   Edited *Nebula Award Stories Eleven* (award-winning science fiction stories). The Earthsea Trilogy (*The Wizard of Earthsea, The Tombs of Atuan,* and *The Farthest Shore*) issued as a collection.

**1978**   Publishes *The Eye of the Heron* and completes *The Language of the Night: Essays on Fantasy and Science Fiction,* which is edited by Susan Wood. Awarded doctorate in literature by Bucknell University.

**1979** *Malafrena* and *Leese Webster* (juvenile novel) published. With mother, Theodora K. Quinn, composes *Tillai and Tylissos* (poetry). Awarded the Gandalf Award (Grand Master of Fantasy) by Worldcon, an annual science fiction convention. Nominated for Balrog Award for best poet.

**1980** Publishes *The Beginning Place* and issues the *Torrey Pines Reserve* (poetry broadsheet). With Virginia Kidd, edits *Interfaces: An Anthology of Speculative Fiction* and *Edges: Thirteen New Tales from the Borderlands of the Imagination.*

**1981** *Hard Words and Other Poems* (poetry) released.

**1982** *The Compass Rose* (short stories) published.

**1983** *In the Red Zone* (poetry) published.

**1984** Wins Locus Award.

**1985** *Always Coming Home* released. Writes *King Dog: A Screenplay,* and with David Bedford, *Rigel Nine: An Audio Opera.*

**1986** A collaboration with composer Elinor Armer, *Uses of Music in Uttermost Parts,* is performed in part in San Francisco, California, and Seattle, Washington.

**1987** *Buffalo Gals and Other Animal Presences* (short stories and poems) published.

**1988** *A Visit from Dr. Katz* and *Catwings* published. *Wild Oats and Fireweed* (poems) released. Travels to England.

**1989** Publishes *Dancing at the Edge of the World: Thoughts on Words, Women, Places* (essays). *Catwings Return* is published.

**1990** *Tehanu: The Last Book of Earthsea* (sequel to *The Farthest Shore*) appears. Produces *Blood Lodge Dances* (dances) with Judy Patton, Christine Bourdette, and others.

**1991** *Searoad: Chronicle of Klatsand* (short stories) released.

**1992**   Produces *Stone Dances* (dances) with Judy Patton, Christine Bourdette, and colleagues. *No Boats* (a chapbook of poetry), *Findings* (a prose chapbook), *Fish Soup* and *A Ride on the Red Mare's Back* (picture books), and *The Language of the Night* (revised essays) published.

**1993**   *Blue Moon over Thurman Street* with photographer Roger Dorband and *The Art of Bunditsu* (prose chapbook) published. Edits *The Norton Book of Science Fiction* with Brian Attebery and Karen Fowler.

**1994**   *Going out with Peacocks* (poetry) and *Wonderful Alexander and the Catwings* (picture/adventure book) released. HarperCollins launches new imprint, HarperPrism, with publication of *A Fisherman of the Inland Sea* (short stories).

**1995**   *Fours Ways to Forgiveness* (science fiction novellas) published.

**1996**   Publishes *Unlocking the Air* (short stories).

# 1. Ursula K. Le Guin: Dancing Weaver

In Ursula K. Le Guin's fiction, spiders are creative souls who toss out connecting threads and find unexpected connections and who trace those touchpoints into patterned webs that appear delicate and ephemeral yet are stronger than tensile steel. Like spiders, Ursula K. Le Guin finds new connections and weaves patterns— lovely, unique, useful—which hold strong to the minds that bump against them. Unlike spiders, Le Guin does anything but sit at the center of her webs and wait. Instead, she dances from web to web, finding and making visible threads that connect crosswise and remind us of new ways to step to ancient melodies. She is wise enough to hear the age-old patterns of humanity, yet her imagination is young and fresh enough to spin out new ways to dance.

It would have been difficult for Ursula K. Le Guin not to have become wise in the ways of human nature. Born on 21 October 1929 in Berkeley, California, and named for her patron saint, she was the youngest child and only daughter of Theodora and Alfred Kroeber, who gave her their own habits of thoughtful scholarship as well as an avid yet respectful curiosity about the differences among human cultures.

Alfred Kroeber (1897–1960) was internationally known for his anthropological work among North American Indians. As the founder of an outstanding Department of Anthropology at the University of California at Berkeley, he welcomed a fascinating variety of acquaintances into his home, ranging from writers and scholars, such as the scientist Robert Oppenheimer, to European refugees and American Indians, who all shared their stories with

1

the family. One special friend was Ishi, the last surviving member of the Yahi tribe of Northern California, who had lived much of his life completely outside the white world. In 1911, he was brought to the Berkeley museum, where Kroeber worked with him until his death in 1916.

Ursula's mother, Theodora Kracaw Kroeber Quinn (1897–1979), a redhead nicknamed "Krakie"[1] from the Colorado mining town of Telluride, met her future husband during her graduate work at Berkeley in 1923. Only twenty-six years old and already in possession of a master's degree in psychology, a widow and the mother of sons Clifton and Theodore, she met and soon married the older, widowed Dr. Kroeber. Karl, another son, was born in 1926, and then Ursula was born in 1929. Le Guin has written that, although her mother may have seemed a conventional wife and mother, she "made her daughter feel a lifelong welcome, giving me the conviction that I had done the right thing in being born a woman" (140). Theodora supported and aided her husband's constant quest for new viewpoints and more knowledge, but she also gained public respect for her own writing achievements. In 1959, at the age of sixty-two, she published *The Inland Whale,* a collection of nine tales about California Indian women. Her next venture was *Ishi in Two Worlds* (1961), a biography of her husband's friend, whose life bridged the nomadic culture of his forest people and the technological modern Western culture of early twentieth-century America. She also wrote several children's books and a biography of her husband, *Alfred Kroeber: A Personal Configuration* (1970).

Clearly, Ursula's sensitivity to the various rhythms and patterns of different ways of thinking and feeling was nourished by her family's conversations with their friends. Ursula paid tribute to her mother in a poem, "To Krakie," she dictated when she was four years old: "Bears like honey / I do too, / I like you, honey / I sure do."[2] Reprinted in *First Words,* the poem indicates her wit and playfulness with language, as well as an early familiarity with the conventions of literature. A year later, when she was five, her brother Ted, "ashamed to discover that he had an illiterate sister" (316), taught her to read and write.

During the academic year, the family lived in a spacious redwood house that faced San Francisco Bay. In the intellectually sophisticated world of Berkeley, Ursula was stimulated by the traditional ideas, music, art, and literature of the Western world. She and her brothers also relied on their imaginations when they played. They collected stuffed animals, establishing an Animal Kingdom, some members of which still live in the Le Guin home. The armadillo sometimes travels with Le Guin; an anteater has been supplied with her own metal ants; and the venerable panda, Austin, serves as doctor emeritus of the Kingdom. Ursula composed a medical textbook for Austin with instructions on "how to repair torn lion hide, and how to stuff sawdust back into a giraffe."[3]

In the summer, the family, and often friends, moved to an overgrown 40-acre ranch in the Napa Valley named Kishamish, a haven where Ursula and her brothers explored the woods and hills with their family friends, among them Juan Dolores, a Papago Indian who visited each year. Summer was a time for reading, swimming, and listening to stories and good talk, often around a campfire under the stars. Ursula writes about hearing her father, the storyteller of the family, retell Indian legends before she learned to read. Ursula remembers the anthropologists who visited as especially "exciting people,"[4] intensely interested in individuals as representatives of their cultures and in the similarities that bound them as humans. Anthropologists practice observing human interactions as objectively as possible, trying to learn about the values and actions of other cultures beyond the traditional prejudices of their own backgrounds. Ursula learned early from her family and their many acquaintances to look beyond the boundaries of a single viewpoint; to carefully listen, watch, and consider alternate views about human morality, human motivations, and the effects humans have on each other and on their environment. These habits of shifting her viewpoints to raise new questions are evident in her thinking.

One of the traditions she challenged later in her writing is the Western tendency to polarize good and evil, light and dark, hero and victim. The ancient Chinese doctrine of Taoism, as described in a favorite book of her father's, the *Tao Te Ching*, encourages a receptive consciousness of the rhythms of nature and an attitude of adjusting to those rhythms rather than conquering them. Le Guin's characters often learn to observe before acting, to let events happen rather than challenge and change them. Her heroes succeed when they learn this wisdom, appreciating the interdependence of action and inaction, light and dark, and even of order and chaos. This is a difficult concept for many readers because Western languages and cultural assumptions are based more on the explicit contrast of opposites than on shared meanings.

Although her books do contain ideas that seem new to many readers, they also reflect traditional themes and values. In her youth, Ursula read widely, especially myths, legends, and fairy tales. She preferred the Norse, "who were always hitting each other with axes ... much more up a kid's alley,"[5] to Greek mythology with its romantic shenanigans. She and her brother also read "trash" as well as the classics, absorbing stories, style, and ideas from them all. Her deep familiarity with the language and stories of various cultural traditions gave her a sense of the themes and images shared by human consciousness.

These universal symbols are called archetypes by Carl Jung, who first articulated the theory of a shared human subconscious, including such personifications as the mother; the divine child or super-hero; the animus and the anima (the masculine and female tendencies, respectively); and the Shadow, or the dark side of human nature. In his theory, humans all share such universal experiences as leaving home, challenging the status quo, and developing a mature identity through rebirth. Le Guin's work reflects her profound understanding of these archetypes, a familiarity bred from the wide range of her cultural literacy rather than from conscious study, although her father corresponded with Jung. Because she embodies these themes in characters whose personalities stretch beyond types and whose adventures are so thoroughly new, they are accessible to modern readers.

In Le Guin's novels, certain values and traits recur. Like herself, her protagonists are curious and observant about their environment. Respectful of cultural differences, they assume a moral obligation to preserve, rather than conquer or destroy, the environments and peoples they travel among. Loyalty to friends, independence, appreciation of music and language, and a love of animals—especially cats—are qualities that often appear as virtues in her characters. These are serious themes and Le Guin is a serious writer. However, her sly sense of humor and quirky imagination also shape her adventures into odd forms and color her characters with characteristics that make even the most alien surprisingly familiar. She has fun when she writes.

As a young girl living in a family who respected new ideas based on careful observation; thoughtful interpretation; and constant learning from listening, reading, and talking, Ursula early on valued the worth of her own perceptions and shared them confidently. Besides reading and participating in family conversations, Ursula wrote stories, including a science fiction story she submitted, unsuccessfully, to *Astounding Stories* when she was 11 years old. Disappointed but not discouraged, she continued to write but did not try to publish for another 10 years.

When Ursula was 12, feeling more like an observer of the typical California adolescence than a participant and afraid her peers would sense her inner differentness (Fadiman, 23), she opened Lord Dunsany's *A Dreamer's Tales* (1910) and was amazed to discover that "people are still making up myths. . . . Whatever the reason, the moment was decisive. I had discovered my native country."[6] By now, she had abandoned science fiction for more traditional literature. She read Tolstoy and Dickens among others and eventually developed an interest in the sources of Western European literature.

In 1947, Ursula enrolled in Radcliffe College, Cambridge, Massachusetts, where she specialized in Renaissance French and Italian literature. As a child, her interests had been biology and poetry, but difficulties with math limited her choices, and she had already decided that her real calling was to write. A serious student, she graduated Phi Beta Kappa in 1951 and enrolled in Columbia University, New York, earning a master's degree in French and Renaissance literature in 1952. In 1953, Ursula, the winner of a Fulbright fellowship, boarded the *Queen Mary*, an ocean liner bound for France. There she met Charles A. Le Guin, a tall, handsome scholar of French history from Macon, Georgia, with a mustache and a southern drawl. "Eet was love, Eet was Paris, Eet was chemistry!" says Le Guin in a 1986 interview (Fadiman, 24). They were married that December in Paris after an autumn of cutting through the knotty red tape foreigners meet when they want to get married in France. Turning to other kinds of learning and writing, Ursula K. Le Guin never finished her doctoral thesis on the poet Jean Lemaire de Belges.

Before her children were born, Le Guin worked as a secretary and taught French at several institutions, including Mercer University in Macon, Georgia, from 1954 to 1955, while her husband worked on his doctorate at Emory University and then finished it at the University of Idaho in 1956. In 1957 their daughter Elisabeth, now a cellist, was born, and in 1959 they had their second daughter, Caroline, who now teaches English at a community college. The family settled in Portland, Oregon, occupying a house built in 1899 in the Thurman Street neighborhood, where they still live. From the children's room where Le Guin now writes, she can see Mt. St. Helens.

In 1993, Le Guin collaborated with photographer Roger Dorband on the book *Blue Moon over Thurman Street* to record the all-American mixture of this street, which runs the "gamut from row house to warehouse to fancy mansion,"[7] and where faces reflect a wide spectrum of ethnic origin, economic status, and life experience.

Most thought-provoking authors write many pages before they are published, and Le Guin is no exception. From 1951 to 1961, she wrote five novels—some of them about an imaginary country, Orsinia—all rejected by publishers because they seemed distant and inaccessible. She also wrote poetry at this time, some of which was published in *Wild Angels* (1975). In addition to writing, she focused energy on her family. She has written that, because of the economic structure in America, she would not have been able to both write and bring up her children without the support of her husband. Besides supporting the family economically as a history professor at Portland State University, her hus-

Ursula K. Le Guin smiles enigmatically from her office, filled with pictures.
*Courtesy of Marian Wood Kolisch.*

band Charles watched over the children when she needed time to finish a story. Despite the difficulties of concentrating on ideas while keeping house and raising young children, she feels that her thinking was enriched by her experiences as a mother.

In 1961, a friend showed her a story in the magazine *Fantasy and Science Fiction* by Cordwainer Smith (the pseudonym of Paul Linebarger) called "Alpha Ralpha Boulevard." The story was romantic science fiction, yet intellectually sophisticated. Impressed, Le Guin renewed her childhood interest in the genre. Another author who inspired her with the philosophic and even prophetic underpinnings of his science fiction was Philip K. Dick. Le Guin decided to emulate these writers. "April in Paris," a fantasy story, was published in 1962 in the magazine *Fantastic,* for which she was paid $30, and "The Masters," a science fiction story, appeared in the same magazine in 1963. Always a competent student, Le Guin taught herself the science she needed for this kind of fiction and eventually developed a sophisticated understanding of many scientific concepts, although she favors anthropology and psychology.

In a recent interview, Le Guin explained that she first chose to write science fiction because "I could sell it and because it has an intelligent readership, and because I like it—I find it beautiful."[8] In recent years, Le Guin has become less patient with the academic definitions of literary genres, which separate "respectable literature" from works and authors who are ignored by college professors and critics. She also dismisses the differentiation between science fiction and fantasy as "elves over here, robots over there" (Fadiman, 23). In a more thorough discussion, she notes the similarities between realism and science fiction as opposed to fantasy: "In science fiction, as in realism, nothing happens that couldn't happen or shouldn't happen. Whereas in fantasy, the contract is just the opposite. The reader agrees to enter the writer's world and follow its laws."[9] Furthermore, mainstream writers of today, such as Italo Calvino, Toni Morrison, Gloria Naylor, and Leslie Silko, are increasingly blurring the parameters of conventional realism. However, critics rarely compare authors and works labeled "science fiction" with the classical canon, nor do college literature surveys include these works. "Good science fiction writers, men and women, are pushed aside. Like women, they are conveniently forgotten. . . . All science fiction is treated as if it were inherently second-class."[10] Despite her feeling that the label causes her work to be viewed with a prejudiced eye by critics and scholars, Le Guin has been quite loyal to the science fiction community and was one of the founding members of the Science Fiction Writers Association. She particularly praises its support of new writers.

The early 1960s were a time of increasing productivity for Le Guin. In 1964, her youngest child and only son, Theodore, now a market researcher, was born. Her writing career began in earnest as she published *Rocannon's World* and *Planet of Exile* in 1966 and *City of Illusions* in 1967, three novels that mix fantasy and science fiction to introduce the Hainish universe, a world Le Guin invented to explore her ideas about human society in a metaphorical context. The novels, considered by critics of science fiction and Le Guin herself as inferior to her later work, haphazardly mix scientific-sounding novelties with mythic elements. Yet the stories are exciting; the characters are more than stereotypes; and the settings are full of foreshadowings of her future ideas.

## Increasing Fame and Respect

In 1968, the Le Guin family traveled through England during her husband's sabbatical year. That year was notable because the first of her four Earthsea novels, *A Wizard of Earthsea,* was published. Each of the novels has won major awards, and the series earned her almost immediate recognition as an outstanding writer. When Le Guin complied with the request of editor Herman Schein of Parnassus to write a book specifically for the 11–17 audience, she had never written particularly for young people before. And, much as she feels about the treatment of science fiction, she resents the trivialization of children's and young adult literature by critics and scholars. "The most childish thing about *A Wizard of Earthsea* is its subject: coming of age." Le Guin acknowledges that, for her, this process continued until after she was 30 years old. Le Guin feels that *A Wizard of Earthsea* is the "best put together book"[11] she has ever written.

## Feminist Sympathies

*The Left Hand of Darkness,* published in 1969, received even more critical acclaim, winning two awards from the Science Fiction Writers Association, a Nebula in 1969 and a Hugo in 1970. Barbara Bucknall calls this story of the icy planet of Gethen Le Guin's "first contribution to feminism"[12] because the planet's androgynous inhabitants live without polarized gender roles. Le Guin posed these questions about gender just as the feminist movement was beginning, exploring these ideas for herself as well as for her readers. In 1971, the second of the Earthsea Cycle appeared, *The Tombs of Atuan,* which describes the classical feminine coming-of-age process. It won the Newbery Honor Book Citation.

With the publication of *The Farthest Shore* in 1971, Le Guin finished the trilogy she had proposed, but she was not yet done with the Earthsea novels. Almost 20 years later, in 1990, she added *Tehanu: The Last Book of Earthsea,* which she wrote to balance the male-dominated tradition of fantasy prevalent in her earlier books. In a 1995 interview, Le Guin explained, "I am a woman writer. I finally learned how to say that when I was in my fifties. I am a woman writer, not an imitation man" (Walsh, 200). She feels that "most of our best writing is being done by women" (Walsh, 196), although literature written by women or that focuses on women characters is still treated as a subgenre of literature.

Le Guin has also supported the feminist movement through her membership in the National Organization for Women (NOW) and the National Abortion Rights Action League. In 1977, while she was writing *The Eye of the Heron,* she discovered feminist literary criticism, which questions the lack of women's voices and experiences in the traditional canon. Her younger daughter, Caroline, a feminist and a specialist in women's studies, helped her reexamine her previous assumptions about the impact of gender roles on social status. After spending the summer of 1985 reading *The Norton Book of Literature by Women,* she finally understood that it was not necessary for her "to write like an honorary man" to write well. "One of the functions of art is to give people the words to know their own experience. There are always areas of vast silence in any culture, and part of an artist's job is to go into those areas and come back from the silence with something to say."[13]

## Living at Peace with the World and Its People

Besides feminism, Le Guin has promoted nonviolence and ecological awareness as solutions to global problems, both in the present and for the future. Throughout the 1960s, she participated in demonstrations against atom bomb testing and then against the war in Vietnam. In the 1968 Oregon primary, she worked for Eugene McCarthy, a leader in the peace movement, and later joined the Women's International League for Peace and Freedom. Her pacifist sympathies are obvious in *The Word for World Is Forest,* which first appeared in 1972 in *Again, Dangerous Visions,* a collection of science fiction stories edited by Harlan Ellison. Published as a novel in 1976, this allegorical commentary on the horrible impact of the military conflict on the people and land in Vietnam, with its fast-paced plot, memorable characterizations, and unforgettable images, earned many honors. It won the Hugo Award for best novella, was a National Book Award finalist, and earned the American Library Association's Best Young Adult Books citation and a place on the *Horn Book* honor list. Because Le Guin feels like she is recording a dreamlike experience when she writes, she suffered much in creating this frightening novel with its irreversible upset of the ecological balance. *The Eye of the Heron* (1978) also addresses the struggle of a peaceful people trying to maintain independence in the face of violent oppressors, and *Always Coming Home* (1986) delineates the destructiveness of the militaristic ethic on those who try to maintain their superiority through competition. This work also condemns the irresponsibility of our current carelessness about the impact of technology on the Earth. Le Guin's belief in the Taoist image of a natural order that changes and grows with time, acting and reacting in turn, may be the root of her aversion to authoritarian-imposed order.

In *The Lathe of Heaven* (1971), George Orr discovers he has the power to change the world through his dreams. Horrified, he consults a psychologist. However, the power-hungry therapist uses George to manipulate the world, with disastrous results. Le Guin further explores the dangers of imposed order in her sympathetic portrayal of anarchism in *The Dispossessed: An Ambiguous Utopia* (1974), in which people who are free from an imposed government cooperate to create a benevolent society rather than compete and claw over each other in the usual chaotic image of anarchy. In 1975 this novel won the Hugo Award, the Jupiter Award (presented by instructors of science fiction in higher education), the Nebula Award, and the Jules Verne Award. In 1976 Le Guin's "The Diary of the Rose," which also pits democratic ideals against oppression, won the Jupiter Award for short stories.

## Wide Range of Expression

"Writing is the only thing besides housework that I really know much about; therefore it is the only thing I feel competent to teach," writes a modest Le Guin in *Dancing at the Edge of the World* (p. vii). Le Guin has practiced her teaching as Writer in Residence or lecturer at such institutions as Mercer University (Idaho), Portland State University (Oregon), Pacific College, Indiana University, Kenyon College, Tulane University, Bennington College, Beloit, Stanford University, and Reading University (England). There she enjoys the opportunity to work in concert with other artists and teachers. As a teacher, she situates herself not as an authoritative source of knowledge but as a partner, participating with and emulating others.

The list of her literary honors stretches long. She has received five Nebula Awards, beginning in 1969 for *The Left Hand of Darkness;* five Hugo Awards; two Jupiter Awards; and a Newbery Silver Medal Award in 1972 for *The Tombs of Atuan.* In the same year, she was a finalist for the National Book Award for Children's Books for *The Farthest Shore.* In 1975, she was a guest of honor at Aussiecon, the World Science Fiction Convention in Melbourne, Australia. The range of her talents was recognized in

1979, when she was awarded the Gandalf Award (Grand Master of Fantasy) at Worldcon, another science fiction convention, and nominated for the Balrog Award for best poet of the year. Other awards include the Locus Award for *The Compass Rose* in 1984, an H. L. Davis Award from Oregon Institute of Literary Arts in 1992, the Hubbub award and *Asimov's* Readers' Award in 1995. She is active professionally, a member of the Authors League, the Writers Guild, the Science Fiction Research Association, and the Science Fiction Poetry Association.

Although Le Guin was first celebrated for her science fiction and fantasy writing, she has expressed her imaginative viewpoints in various literary formats. *Very Far Away from Anywhere Else* (1976) is a realistic love story, a short novel that portrays two gifted young people who find the kind of love that allows both the liberty to develop their gifts. *Malafrena* (1979) is a historical novel taking place in early nineteenth-century Orsinia, an imaginary European country that appears in other novels and short stories. *The Beginning Place* (1980) uses elements of magic realism, interweaving the everyday with the extraordinary as a romance develops between two lonely teenagers who escape from their bleak tawdry world into a fantasy land.

*Searoad: Chronicle of Klatsand* (1992) uses self-confessional monologues to reveal the private thoughts of several generations of women living in a small seaside town. In *A Fisherman of the Inland Sea* (1994), Le Guin returns to the use of science fiction imagery to explore individual minds. *Four Ways to Forgiveness* (1995) is a collection of four interconnected novellas, again crossbreeding elements of science fiction with psychological realism; the borders are increasingly smudged as Le Guin portrays individual characters of the Hainish universe so personally that the reader feels more connections than differences.

Le Guin's many short stories range widely in genre from science fiction, fantasy, retellings of fairy tales, feminism, magic realism, and straight-out realism. Several have been collected in single volumes: *The Wind's Twelve Quarters* (1975) includes some fantasy and science fiction stories; the stories of *Orsinian Tales* (1976) take place in the imaginary eastern European land mentioned above; *The Compass Rose* (1982) and the *Buffalo Gals* collections (1987, 1994) contain both short stories and poems. *Unlocking the Air* (1996), her newest collection of short fiction, stretches the outer edge of the usual definition of reality, releasing what has been previously difficult to articulate.

Le Guin's books of poetry include *Wild Angels* (1975); a volume written with her mother, Theodora Kroeber Quinn, *Tillai and Tylissos* (1979); a poetry broadsheet, *Torrey Pines Reserve* (1980); *Hard Words and Other Poems* (1981); *In the Red Zone* (1983); *Wild Oats and Fireweed* (1988); a chapbook, *No Boats* (1992); *Blue Moon over Thurman Street* (1993) with photographer Roger Dorband; and *Going out with Peacocks* (1994). As much as her poetry can be classified, it tends to be lyrical and imagistic, focusing on the sounds of the mind reacting to nature and the images that connect the human and "natural" worlds, erasing traditional boundaries between the two.

Le Guin is quite outspoken about her thoughts and her processes of composing and writing. Her ideas are gathered in several collections of critical essays: *Dreams Must Explain Themselves* (1975); *The Language of the Night: Essays on Fantasy and Science Fiction* (1979), edited by Susan Wood, and *Dancing at the Edge of the World: Thoughts on Words, Women, Places* (1989). Because she is interested in encouraging thought-provoking writers, Le Guin has edited several collections, including *Interfaces: An Anthology of Speculative Fiction* (1980) and *Edges: Thirteen New Tales from the Borderlands of the Imagination* (1980), with Virginia Kidd, and *The Norton Book of Science Fiction* (1993), with Brian Attebery and Karen Fowler.

Le Guin has also written several children's books. *Leese Webster* (1979), illustrated by James Brunsman, is a picture book about a spider whose creative cobwebs get framed in a museum, forcing her to move outside to survive. In 1982 she wrote both *The Adventures of Cobbler's Rune* and *Adventures in Kroy*. Le Guin's love of cats, especially the winged variety she invented for *Rocannon's World,* is evident in *Catwings* (1988), *Catwings Return* (1989), and *Wonderful Alexander and the Catwings* (1994), all illustrated by S. D. Schindler. *A Ride on the Red Mare's*

*Back* (1992) is a legend about the red-painted, wooden toy Dalarna horse from Sweden, a tale inspired by her trip to that country. Other books include *Solomon Leviathan* (1988), illustrated by Alicia Austin; *A Visit from Dr. Katz* (1988), illustrated by Ann Barrow; *Fire and Stone* (1989), illustrated by Laura Marshall; and *Fish Soup* (1992), illustrated by Patrick Wynne.

Le Guin's continual exploration of different ways of telling stories led her to experiment with various media. In 1979 she worked on the television production of *The Lathe of Heaven,* and in 1981 the extraordinary short story, "The Ones Who Walk Away from Omelas" was performed with dance and music at the Portland Civic Theatre. With choreographer Judy Patton and designer Christine Bourdette, among others, Le Guin composed two other dances: *Blood Lodge Dances* (1990) and *Stone Dances* (1992). She has enjoyed collaborating with other artists as a welcome change from the solitude of writing. *Rigel Nine: An Audio Opera* (1985) was written with composer David Bedford. *Always Coming Home* (1985), a multimedia interpretation of Le Guin's futuristic version of life on the American Pacific Coast, includes illustrations by Margaret Chodos, diagrams by George Hersh, and a tape cassette of "Music and Poetry of the Kesh," with music by Todd Barton. Although she claims to be "musically ignorant," Le Guin believes that written words can be perceived like music or speech when listeners pay attention to them as an "event" existing outside the mind (Commire, 111). In 1986, she teamed up with composer Elinor Armer in a series of text-and-music works, *Uses of Music in Uttermost Parts,* which have been performed numerous times and appeared as a double CD for Koch International in 1995. In her works, Le Guin pushes out the borders of all kinds of literary traditions. She is a true scientist of expression, experimenting widely and deeply. In her essay "Dreams Must Explain Themselves," Le Guin explains that she discovers people and places rather than invents them.

Except when she is attending conventions or teaching, her life is quiet; she writes every day she can, beginning at seven or eight in the morning. She reads widely in a variety of subjects related to her writing. The authors whom she has mentioned as influences include Percy Bysshe Shelley, Victor Hugo, William Butler Yeats, Theodore Roethke, and Lucille Clifton among poets, and Charles Dickens, Lev Tolstoy, Boris Pasternak, Virginia Woolf, Lao Tzu, Italo Calvino, and Jorges Borges among novelists. Among science fiction writers, she especially appreciates Philip K. Dick, about whom she wrote "The Modest One" (1976). Despite her claims to the contrary, Le Guin is quite knowledgeable about music. She and her husband frequently attend concerts, and their eldest daughter, Elisabeth, is a professional cellist. Le Guin has played the recorder for much of her life, though she does not claim any great talent for it. Images of music and dance appear frequently in her works; she writes about singing and dancing, she says, as recompense for her lack of actual expertise in either.

Her relationship to the physical activities she describes in her writing, such as skiing, snowshoeing, and even driving, is similar to the many images of sailing in her work, particularly in the Earthsea Trilogy. Her descriptive powers are based on imagination rather than actual experience with these sports. In a letter, she describes a spectacular sailing adventure that bears little resemblance to the graceful skimming journeys of her fictional sailors. She and a friend took a sailing lesson that ended abruptly as their craft overturned in barely enough water; the two would-be sea captains celebrated by intoning the hymn, "Nearer My God to Thee," while their instructor nearly wept.

What is Ursula K. Le Guin like as a person? Trim and of medium height, her large eyes reflect in turn her somber concern about modern humanity's violence against the very matter and natural rhythms of our world and, in contrast, a merry playfulness; she looks like she knows the world enough to be both worried and amused. Now in her sixties, "her face is fretted with laugh lines; she has almost no frown lines" (Fadiman, 25). For most of her life, she has worn her now silvering hair in a short style that reporters describe as pixieish or elfish. She is an elegant woman with a ready sense of humor. Invited to make a keynote speech at the bastion of academic dignity and tradition, Oxford University in England, Le Guin appeared in an eminently appropriate black wool suit, but capped by a beanie topped with a propeller. Her letters and essays are written so naturally that the reader easily hears the spirited brightness of a mind that knows both the pleasures of ordering a house and spinning scholarly images. She continues to campaign against the exclusiveness of many literary critics who insist on proclaiming the superiority of the traditional canon over science fiction; fantasy; or literature marketed for children, young adults, or women. People who think that they can write books for children in their spare time are "incredibly arrogant," she claims; "[c]hildren's literature is as tight a discipline as writing poetry" (Walsh, 194).

A knowledgeable and sophisticated literary critic herself, she nevertheless has teased the pretentious members of academia by selecting "Mom de Plume" as a pseudonym.[14] Her writing is full of jokes and lyrics, slang and poetry; her subject matter ranges from practical advice about replacing fuel-guzzling air and auto travel with a system of trains[15] to theoretical analysis of the meanings of narrative forms, complete with the most respectable scholarly references. In the poem "Places," describing a cross-country trip from her home in Oregon to visit her husband's relatives in Macon, she revels in the weird place names and complains about the heat. A real, whole, complex person emerges from her writing, who gently mocks us for our human foibles as she tries to save our world from destruction.

Le Guin is considered a major American writer and literary influence by many literary critics, as well as by readers who eagerly await her latest creations to see what new directions she will take as she explores basic questions about the human heart, mind, and spirit. By now, she is an expert at taking the reader from territory that seems ordinary and familiar to new places, always surprising but no longer alien. Each story she writes, each new work, is a great adventure, a "thought experiment" to use her term, in which trusting readers learn to follow her lead, jumping among networks of ideas, images, lyrics, and possibilities.

# 2. Learning the Hainish Dance: *Rocannon's World, Planet of Exile,* and *City of Illusions*

Ursula K. Le Guin began her publishing career writing science fiction, now called speculative fiction, and has consistently been labeled a "science fiction" writer since. Although she has regretted the limited critical acceptance of science fiction as serious literature, she has repeatedly defended it as a genre that allows freedom to speculate on or explore the "real" world using imagery and patterns she finds beautiful. The imaginary world is one that literary taste–mongers have ignored. She hopes that the current tendency to melt borders between literary forms, particularly by such prominent writers as Margaret Atwood and Doris Lessing, will erase the traditional prejudices toward speculative fiction (Dezell, 70). The kinds of images used in science fiction, as in myth, effectively raise pivotal issues about human society to consciousness by embodying these issues in a story form more complex than mere explanation allows. Le Guin recognizes the value of science fiction as a way to "face an open universe. Physically open, psychically open. No doors shut."[1] Although Le Guin has called her early novels "fairy tales decked out in space suits,"[2] they introduce many of the most effective metaphors and conceptual frameworks of her later works. Even these early works reflect her interest in exploring the implications of legends and myths for current beliefs and behaviors and in using imagined technology to comment on social and political organizations and their effects on relationships between individuals. More than extrapolation, which attempts to predict the future by supposing a single change or exaggeration of our present situation, Le Guin's "thought experiments" create worlds with unique histories and myths, which extend and expand ordinary assumptions about how living beings coexist with the physical world. These three early novels contain the beginning steps of her sojourn into the mythic world of the Hainish.

Readers meet the Hainish not on their home planet of Hain, or Davenant, but on other worlds as they assiduously explore their universe. Elizabeth Cummins points out that the Hainish myth retells the "story of human expansion"[3] as the inhabitants of the universe struggle to find ways to coexist despite differing cultural goals, traditions, and languages. Le Guin did not plan the Hainish world and its history from the start but discovered it as she wrote, moving back and forth in time as she set her mind in different directions. Like an anthropologist who pieces together a story of a people from artifacts and legends as well as from current behaviors, Le Guin leads her readers along imaginative paths rather than provide a fully painted textbook history from the start. However, both Ian Watson[4] and James Bittner[5] have worked out chronologies, which most other critics accept as valid, for Le Guin's Hainish history. Of the major Hainish novels, the most recently published, *The Dispossessed* (1974), is set the earliest, in 2300 A.D., and focuses on the inhabitants of a colonized planet. One short story, "The Day Before the Revolution" (1974), precedes this novel in the Hainish timeline. It is told from the viewpoint of Odo, a charter member of the colonizing society but a woman too old to fully enjoy the enthusiasm of the young settlers. This story describes the Hainish as the oldest known people, "meditative . . . civil, considerate, rather somber,"[6] and altruistic, actively working to establish peaceful coexistence among the planets. Their concern for unity seems motivated by lessons learned over the long span of their experience. They rescued the Terrans of Earth "gently, charitably, as the strong man treats the sick one" (347). The mindlessly greedy, carelessly violent human beings of Earth have made it a desert, killing its forests and large animals and turning its skies gray. Surviving only by totally centralizing and controlling their resources, they were helped by the Hainish, who gave them spaceships to leave their "ruined world" (348).

Although not usually designated as part of the Hainish series, *The Lathe of Heaven* (1971) paints a horrifying picture of the destruction of Earth, saved by the beneficial invasion of aliens, who, in the shape of sea turtles, act with the same rational morality as the Hainish. Tragically, however, by 2368 A.D., the Terrans have rallied enough to transport their poisonous habits to the colony Athshe, which they systematically destroy in *The Word for World Is Forest* (1976). In response, the Hainish form the League of All Worlds to establish peaceful interplanetary communication for trade and education. A device, called the ansible, which enables planets to communicate messages across the light-year distances of space without losing time was made possible by the work of Shevek, the Cetian physicist whose story is told in *The Dispossessed*. In the early days of the League, however, the ansible's functioning was slow. Explorers who traveled beyond the reliable range were quite isolated. Le Guin describes the panic of being lost in a completely foreign world in the short story "Vaster Than Empires and More Slow," written in 1971 and included in the collection *The Wind's Twelve Quarters* (1975). In this story, a group of Terrans are seeking new planets to explore, like adolescents wanting to escape the familiar and the secure, in this case, the Hainish who "like tiresomely understanding parents"[7] fund these unreasonable rebellious members of their family.

In the first three of her published science fiction novels, Le Guin describes the early days of the loosely formed League. The books in this early trilogy refer to enemies who threaten their security. In *Rocannon's World* (1966), set in 2684, the hero avenges companions who died in an explosion. On a different planet a millennium later in 3755, the Alterrans of *Planet of Exile* (1966) have been abandoned for generations, their ship either lost or still engaged in battle with an enemy to the League. In *City of Illusions* (1967), which occurs in 4370, the enemy is identified as the evil Shing, whose truth-shattering power must be destroyed so the League can be restored. By 4870, the time of "Winter's King" (1969) and *The Left Hand of Darkness* (1969), the League has evolved into a cooperative organization of 83 worlds called the Ekumen, complete with Ekumenical proverbs and laws. One important law is the Cultural Embargo, which maintains that visitors to other planets not introduce more advanced technology, so as to avoid tainting native cultures, but this law is often disobeyed. The federation of planets provides a familiar background to readers of these science fictions, which share a common linguistic source; labels such as HILFs (highly intelligent life forms); and assumed values such as mutual trading of information and services, cultural and environmental preservation, and protection from invasive colonization. These same principles are also evident outside the Hainish universe, in *Always Coming Home,* written almost two decades after Le Guin's first speculative fictions.

## *Rocannon's World*

"How can you tell the legend from the fact on these worlds that lie so many years away?—planets without names, called simply The World, planets without history, where the past is the matter of myth, and a returning explorer finds his own doings of a few years back have become the gestures of a god."[8] These first lines of Le Guin's first published book introduce questions about the effect of naming in particular and of language in general on defining and understanding fact. In the minds of many young readers, what is named "history" is more valid and useful than myth. Yet, as historical records multiply, the meaning or long-term impact of what happens is often buried in detail. Throughout her work, Le Guin questions the completeness of truth authorized as scientific fact or official history; she incorporates newly imagined names, words, devices for traveling and communicating, racial and ethnic divisions, and political justifications in order to cause readers to stretch their minds beyond traditional linear interpretations. This introduction to her work serves as fair warning.

*Rocannon's World* begins with "Semley's Necklace," a short story also published as "Dowry of the Angyar" in 1964 and considered by Le Guin as "her first science fiction story that begins to break from the trivial" (Commire, 105). This story is reprinted in *The Wind's Twelve Quarters* (1975). It is loosely based on the Norse myth of Freya, whose greed for gold drives her to leave her young daughter and husband to seek a golden necklace. She agrees to spend a night with dwarves who, much to her disgust, fondle her all night before showing her where to satisfy her desire for the beautiful necklace. When she returns home, she finds that her husband is gone and her daughter has grown to adulthood during her absence. Le Guin modifies the legend somewhat, broadening the psychological explanation for the woman's greed and examining the social status of these dwarflike peoples. Semley wants the golden necklace so she can compete with wealthier women and live up to her husband's noble reputation. The dwarf society includes both the Fiia, delicate elfish creatures, attractive yet unproductive, and the heavier Clayfolk, who excel at making things. The story adds resonance to the journey of the novel's title character, justifying his initial loyalty to Mogien, his host and best informant.

The scientifically minded Starlords from the League of All Worlds, known as the Strangers, have sent Rocannon, the Director of the First Ethnographic Survey, on an eight-year time travel journey to Fomalhaut II, an oxygen-rich planet in Galactic Area 8. Rocannon, a 43-year-old, white-skinned, dark-haired ethnologist, has the thoughtful manners, the habit of careful observation, the sensitivity for the nuances of communication, and the appreciation for different cultures that come from his lifelong interest in studying different peoples. Typical of several of Le Guin's later protagonists, he comes unencumbered by material goods, carrying only a map of the planet, an invisible impermasuit that protects him from injury and cold, and a guidebook.

His *Abridged Handy Pocket Guide to Intelligent Life-Forms* identifies four possible groups of highly intelligent life forms (hilfers) on Fomalhaut II as fully humanoid. The first people he meets are, in scientific terms, Species II, also called Liuar. These tall folk live in the misty cold northern mountains in an environment much like medieval northern Europe. The Angyar, or lords, are attractive, dark skinned, and golden haired and live in drafty stone castles with walls covered with tapestries and furniture of stone and heavy wood. Proud and imperious, enthusiastic in battle, they are served by the Olgyior, middle-sized serfs with white skin and dark hair like Rocannon. As in medieval European societies, family bloodlines matter and mixed marriages are frowned upon. The Olgyior take oaths of loyalty to the Angyar noblemen, pledging "to give the hours of my life and the use of my death" (*Rocannon*, 75). Le Guin later wrote more extensively about this European-like aristocratic pride in novels such as *Malafrena* and *The Eye of the Heron*.

Less civilized in the traditional sense of the word are the Gdemiar, or Clayfolk, who are Species I: A. These people live underground in minelike caves made habitable by highly developed technology. Nocturnal, short, pale-skinned troglodytes with dank dark hair, they are highly talented craftspeople who feel that their cleverness is unappreciated by the beautiful "takers," the Angyar, for whom they make jewelry and swords. Because of their technical superiority, the League has chosen to develop the Gdemiar, providing them with further knowledge and a spaceship for easy travel. The Gdemiar, who both give and take, communicate in a voice that seems to come from no individual, a sort of generic voice that seems creepy to Rocannon. This means of communication may be a precursor to mindspeech, a form of telepathy used more extensively in several later novels.

Belonging to the same species but choosing to live in light rather than darkness are the Fiia, small, delicate, fair-skinned and fair-haired beings who live in the sunlit valleys. Like the Clayfolk, they also possess the talent for mindspeech or communicating without direct speech, but the effect is different. These gentle sprites avoid the precise naming and defining of technology, communicating mood more than specific information. In assigning social status and power to these ethnic divisions, Le Guin overturns the traditional preference in Western culture for light-skinned European racial attributes, a device she repeats in many later works where the main characters' dark-skinned Negroid features are considered most attractive and normal. She also establishes various motivations for competition and resentment among ethnic groups that she explores more deeply in later novels. The Angyars' ethnocentric pride in their traditions recurs throughout her work in peoples who consider themselves masters. Just as often, her writings depict gentle, nonaggressive cultures like that of the Fiia, who desire peace and independence more than power.

Rocannon communicates with his home planet by means of the ansible, a radio device that sends messages across the boundaries of both time and space, so that they arrive instantly. Le Guin uses this device again in *City of Illusions, The Word for World Is Forest,* and especially *The Dispossessed.* The impermasuit she never used again, admitting that it was merely convenient without adding any profound symbolic meaning.

*Rocannon's World* also introduces Le Guin's chronic fondness for cats. She lovingly describes the windsteeds as overgrown cats with wings, which the Angyar ride on the wind over the fields of Kirien. These animals contentedly purr, especially when someone scratches their ears, and they prefer the warmth of sunlight. Afraid or annoyed, their fur rises. They hate water, and when left outside at night, like all good house cats, they scratch and complain until someone pays attention. Le Guin would later indulge her fondness for flying cats in a series of children's stories.

This first novel, patterned on the traditional heroic adventure, presages Le Guin's complex exploration of the metaphor of journey as necessary for becoming a mature, thinking human. In the end, although Rocannon has achieved his outward goal—defeating his enemies, the Faradayans—he suffers inwardly, losing his friend Mogien and sharing the pain of his enemies through mind-speech, which forces him to empathize with his victims rather than celebrate his victory. He learns that conquest is more complex than the simple concept of good versus evil; in war, there are no ultimate winners, even in science fiction.

## *Planet of Exile*

Le Guin's second published novel continues the theme of the dangerous racial prejudices evident in *Rocannon's World*. Originally the League of All Worlds had sent a colony from Rokanan to the planet Askatevar, but now, 10 Askatevarran years later (about 650 Earth years), the 2,000 survivors are stranded in their city, Landin, which is located on the coast, is protected by a huge seastack, and is connected to the mainland by a causeway high above the beach where the tides rush in periodically. These technologically sophisticated, black-skinned colonists practice mindspeech, an ability to communicate as well as understand each other without audible sound, but a law of the League forbids them from tainting other cultures by teaching these skills. They even have a genetic immunity against infections. Nearby, in underground cavelike dwellings, live the native Tevarans, paler-skinned with almond eyes, who know nothing of technology, songs, mindspeech, or other worlds. Each group considers the other subhuman, and both are threatened by the marauding Gaals, a pale-skinned, gray-eyed horde from the North who are fleeing the first winter in 60 years. Curious about the colonists in Landin, Rolery, a young daughter of the aging Tevaran leader Wold, walks to the Tower, where she meets their leader, Jakob Agat Alterra, who inadvertently uses mindspeech in his effort to save her from being washed away by the in-rushing tide. Agat visits Wold the next day to arrange a concerted military effort to ward off the approaching Gaals. Although Wold reluctantly agrees, the younger Tevaran leaders are less willing to overcome their traditional distaste for the colonists. When Jakob Agat and Rolery agree to a love tryst, the warriors avenge this breach of cultural prejudice by attacking Jakob. Drawn by his mindspeech call, Rolery finds him and delivers him half alive to the colonists' city; they marry soon after.

When the Gaal destroy the Tevarans' winter city, Jakob, with the help of the repentant Tevaran leader Umaksuman, rescues the survivors and leads them to the colonists' city. As the Gaal attacks continue, the children and young women are sent to the Tower, but Rolery and other older women remain in the city to help. While she is tending the wounded, she notes that some of the colonists seem to be suffering from infection, which was supposedly not genetically possible. When she tells the doctor, he starts to dismiss her observation but then realizes that the colonists exhibit other signs of evolutionary adjustment; the logical conclusion is that the two races are growing alike and capable of bearing children together. This is welcome news not only to Jakob and Rolery, but to all of the survivors, who now need to work and live together to survive the 5,000 days and nights of Winter.

Le Guin's characters reflect her own moral thinking, as indicated in her essays. Like Rocannon, Jakob is sensible, well-disciplined, and loyal to the League as long as its laws seem practical to him; more than strict obedience to tradition and law, he values tolerance of differences and the ultimate unification of humans. Rolery, while she does not rebel against the conventional female role, is proud and spirited, a strong and naturally independent woman. Le Guin has indicated that Rolery reflects her Taoist belief in the efficacy of "action through stillness" in situations where action seems pointless (Bucknall, 24). As other critics have noted, Le Guin's depiction of the Tevaran leader Wold is one of her most poignant. As his authority over his warriors declines, so does his memory and his ability to focus his attention, but his wry humor and earthy wisdom remain. When he dies at the end of the battle with the Gaals, the women and children cut their hair and smudge their faces in mournful sorrow. Jakob Agat and the other colonists are allowed to join them in expressing their grief, signifying their future unity.

## City of Illusions

A product of that unity is the hero of this final book of the trilogy. Ramarren, a descendant of Agat and Rolery, with the same golden catlike eyes as Rolery's people, is a navigator on an Alterran (as the combined culture is now called) spaceship bound for Earth.

The crew's mission is to reconnect with the League of All Worlds, from which the Alterrans have heard nothing for years. As Ramarren enters planetary space, his mind is erased, and he lands on Earth with no memory and thus no childhood.

The book opens with the dramatic imperative: "Imagine darkness."[9] Then follows a frighteningly vivid description of what it would feel like to live without language, unable to name and classify and make patterns of the chaotic bombardment of sensations in this dark forest where he has landed. A lovely woman named Parth rescues the confused man. A weaver, she brings order to his world by naming him Falk and tutoring him in the language and ways of her culture, including the Canon, which is similar to the Taoist way, and mindspeech.

It is 4370 A.D., and the present civilization of the United States has faded into a series of tribes in a sparsely populated land. Isolation has resulted in vastly different cultures, a scenario Le Guin explores in greater detail in *Always Coming Home*. Fortunately for the navigator Ramarren, he has landed near a gentle extended family who practice the "clean serene frugality" (13) of communal living. Le Guin seems to admire this way of life in other works, most notably in *The Dispossessed* and *Always Coming Home*, in which humans live with a minimum amount of intrusive technology and therefore impose only slightly on the nonhuman environment.

One of Le Guin's favorite inventions is the patterning frame, a wire and bead contraption that imitates a mind's content and ascertains the probable trend of the near future, somewhat like the function of the Patterner in the Earthsea series. It is this patterning frame that helps Parth and her family sense the emptiness of Falk's mind, blank as the eyes of the blind Kreteyn, Parth's cousin and part of the communal household whose master is Zove. After six years, the community decides that the stranger they know as Falk must travel to the city Es Toch to face the enemy Shing and find the keys to his lost identity.

Armed with a laser gun, protected by the light, weatherproof cloth and the potent medicines of this technologically advanced culture, Falk sets forth on foot toward the west through the bleak cold Le Guin favors as settings for unpleasant journeys. The first humans Falk meets show him the cruelty of men who fear; after beating him and questioning him, they drive him off at gunpoint. He slogs on alone, increasingly embittered by his hunger, the constant cold, and the memory of the injunction, "Trust no one," delivered to him by his first host, Tove. His next adventure is kinder. A solitary old man, a listener so empathetic he knows Falk's mind almost before Falk does, gives him sanctuary for three days. But the Listener also warns Falk not to trust anyone. He sends him off with a slider, a vehicle that speeds his pace by gliding above the ground. This invention allows Le Guin to indulge her humorous vein as she describes how Falk learns by trial and error to control this handy machine. Just as he gets cocky, wondering at the pessimism of the people he has met, he is shot down again, by a male-dominated tribe of Hunters whose lives revolve around sex, meat, and machismo. This time he is saved by the red-haired woman Estrel, who helps him escape during a snow storm. Strangely passive yet also seductive, she fascinates Falk, and he convinces her to accompany him to Es Toch. Together, they undergo many hardships, helping each other in turn to overcome the seemingly insurmountable obstacles of a long journey. However, when they arrive at their destination, it becomes clear that Estrel has been employed by the Shing to lead Falk to them. She convinces him that the Shing, so maligned by Parth's family, are actually beneficent. But the Shing betray his newly founded trust.

Using drugs, the Shing try to dredge his memory for the exact location of his home planet so they can invade it. Orry, a young boy and the only other survivor of the expedition from Tevaran, tells Falk that his real name is Ramarren and helps him regain the story of his origins. Now Falk-Ramarren must decide whom to trust. Deeply betrayed by Estrel, who now appears in androgynous clothing, Falk-Ramarren struggles to achieve harmony between both halves of his mind. It is the first chapter of the Canon (or the *Tao Te Ching*, which Le Guin uses as the basis for much of her thought), that helps Falk-Ramarren connect his knowledge of these men and his technical abilities. The chapter warns that the name he knows is not the whole truth; it is only that part of his self that cannot be named either as solely Falk or Ramarren that will help him sense the truth. The innate courtesy Falk has shown Estrel has affected her enough that she gives him back his Earthly name (Falk) and mistrust of the Shing; his intelligence as Ramarren allows him to work the spaceship and escape. As a whole man, he will be able to warn his home planet of the enemy's intentions. Le Guin's exploration of the ambiguous nature of truth in this novel presages both the importance of knowing true names in *A Wizard of Earthsea* and the strength of loyalty in *The Left Hand of Darkness*.

Le Guin describes the Shing as "the least convincing lot of people I ever wrote," explaining that real villains, characters who intend evil, are rare individuals. Ascribing evil to a group is unrealistic. She credits (or blames) her invention of the Shing to her conversation with her young daughter Elisabeth, who named them and described them only as "bad!" (vi). Wholly evil people are concepts of immature minds who lack the experience and wisdom to see beyond superficial stereotypes and comprehend the inextricable mixture of light and shadow that makes most of Le Guin's characters realistically memorable. Yet the Shing are like Le Guin's other tyrants, whose evil consists of taking "choice and freedom from men" and "stop[ping] the evolution of the race" (17). For Le Guin, the independence to choose one's work and to seek knowledge freely are greater priorities than security or material wealth. Any tendency to unnecessarily limit the choices of other humans or impinge on the life of nonhumans is bad.

Le Guin has criticized her own work, accusing herself of "promiscuous mixing," especially in regard to the invention of the impermasuit, a "good example of how fantasy and science fiction don't shade gracefully into one another."[10] New inventions need to incorporate deeper symbolic meanings to succeed. If they are "merely decorative or convenient ... [they] confuse possibility with probability and end up as neither."[11] Yet these three novels all contain imagery that moves the heart by eliciting scenes of gentle tenderness and that engages the intellect by mining fresh new ideas. Parts of these novels are better than their wholes.

Most of the ideas and images introduced appear later, deepened and broadened to create fuller effects. Le Guin's speculative fiction supposes a world in which ethnic and gender differences are more attractive than repellent, where people notice and appreciate the gifts of both technology and nature. In her fiction, she urges humans to develop these concepts thoughtfully into a life where all beings can coexist peacefully and constructively, following the rhythms of life and death, action and passivity, which she sees as inherent in our universe.

Le Guin is a tremendously prolific writer, not only as judged by the quantity of material she has produced or the number of stylistic forms she uses but by the range of her imagination. In her work, she poses questions and supposes answers from many positions and viewing distances, moving from the universal distance of myth and legend, which asks about the nature and rhythms of life and death, to the political questions about beneficial social relationships of humans, and finally, to queries about the inner workings of individual minds. In her best work, Le Guin weaves these viewpoints into a multidimensional experience in which the personal, the political, and the philosophic are understood as a piece, simultaneously felt, comprehended, and imagined by the whole mind—emotionally, intellectually, and spiritually. These first science fictions are experiments in the kinds of language that move beyond the merely scientific or logical language of explanation into the more comprehensive world of story and legends, and they introduce the Hainish world, which Le Guin used as a metaphor for human endeavors even 30 years later.

# 3. The Earthsea Cycle, a New Dance for Legendary Tunes: *A Wizard of Earthsea,* *The Tombs of Atuan,* *The Farthest Shore,* and *Tehanu*

In the Earthsea Cycle, Ursula K. Le Guin explores the rhythms of the legendary heroic journey. Her heroes venture from a familiar childhood environment toward the new discoveries of adolescence. In adulthood, they recognize and return to some of the wisdoms learned in childhood. In these four books, the protagonists learn the lessons of courage and humility and the art of balancing active seeking with quiet obedience to the universal rhythms. Le Guin is tracing these lessons in the language of fantasy, which views life from a mythic distance, posing philosophic questions about the meanings and purposes of lives with all the beauty, humor, and grace of imaginative storytelling. The main characters in these novels are heroic, chosen to live for the sake of more than themselves, privileged but also burdened with symbolic weight. Yet Le Guin also draws them with faults, foibles, and quirks that make these characters ordinary and alive—someone the reader can care about.

## A Wizard of Earthsea

"Le Guin's Earthsea Cycle is considered a major achievement in fantasy literature, comparable in stature to such popular works as J. R. R. Tolkien's *Lord of the Rings* and C. S. Lewis's *Chronicles of Narnia.*"[1] Such high praise would certainly have amazed Ursula K. Le Guin in 1968 when Houghton published the first of this series, *A Wizard of Earthsea,* as she had received little recognition for previous works. But this novel, with its illustrations by Ruth Robbins, was immediately popular, winning the *Boston Globe Horn Book* Award in 1969, the Lewis Carroll Shelf Award in 1979, and honor citations by *Horn Book* and the American Library Association.

Le Guin wrote *A Wizard of Earthsea* at the request of Herman Schein, an editor at Parnassus Press, who wanted a book for young adults, an audience she had never addressed before. This was an opportunity to think about her own adolescence, which she claims to have finished only after the age of 30. As she explored the process of becoming a whole or mature person, she discovered in her imagination the islands, their magic, and the idea of a college for preservice wizards. "I did not deliberately invent Earthsea. I am not an engineer, but an explorer," she writes. "The story of the book is essentially a voyage, a pattern in the form of a long spiral."[2] The shape of this journey reflects a common theme in Le Guin's works, the completion of an outward venture by returning to the beginning place, but not as the same person.

The first character we meet is Ged. In *The Language of the Night,* Le Guin explains that she "listened" hard for the name that seemed right for the character she was imagining. The name is pronounced with a hard "g" as in "get" and is not meant to evoke any other meaning. "One man ... thought 'Ged' was meant to suggest 'God,'"[3] but this was not what she intended. Names are important in this book, for Le Guin feels that to know the true name of something is to learn the truth of its being, as artists and wizards know things beyond their simple definitions.

This boy, born in a mountain village on the island of Gont in a land called Earthsea, was first given the name Duny by his mother, who died soon after. "Loud, proud, and full of temper" (2), Duny learns spells from his aunt, a simple woman who recognizes his power and teaches him all the magic she knows, including the word to call down sparrowhawks, a talent that brings him the nickname "Sparrowhawk." Even these simple spells prove useful when Duny saves the village in a battle with the savage Gonts by concealing the villagers in a fog until all the enemy is killed. Spent by using so much of his power, he lies dazed until the Mage of Albi, Ogion the Silent, descends from the mountain and cures him. A few months later, on Duny's thirteenth birthday, Ogion bestows upon him his true name, Ged, and adopts him as an apprentice.

Ged is disappointed as he follows his new master's trek through the valleys and over the mountain, for he feels he is learning nothing. After they reach Ogion's modest home at Re Albi, Ged spends the winter months reading the runes and lore of the Hardic language, but he is still impatient; he had expected to learn magic spells to amaze people. His pride is further injured when he meets a young girl who dares him to work a transformation spell. Ashamed of his ignorance, he seeks this glamorous knowledge in a book his master has not shared with him. As he ponders the rune, a "shapeless clot of shadow darker than the darkness" appears, paralyzing Ged with horror. At this moment Ogion returns home and dispels the horror, but Ged's shame remains.

In the traditional archetypal imagery described by Jung, the Shadow often represents the darker, destructive side of the self, which most people try to ignore or suppress. Ogion explains that the power to create different forms by magic or by art includes destructive abilities. Mages, artists, people with power must use care.

Like many adolescents who leave their first teachers to try something different and new, Ged decides to attend the school for mages at Roke when Ogion kindly offers him this choice. There, studying under the Archmage, Nemmerle, he finds himself among other young boys who already know more than he. Like many young people with special gifts, Ged is socially awkward, with a stiff pride that keeps him apart from his peers. He has been a big fish in a small pond; now he feels like a minnow among mackerel, especially when he compares his provincial ways with the urbane habits of another student, Jasper. Ged sets himself up as Jasper's rival. But he is also welcomed by Vetch, a boy whose magical skills are surpassed by his innate kindness, and is befriended by one of the several small furry animals invented by Le Guin; this one, called an otak, becomes Ged's familiar (an animal that acts as a spiritual guide and friend to a person with magical power).

Fascinated by the many powers of magic, Ged quickly becomes adept in all manner of spells. Like Ogion, the Master Hand, a teacher of magical tricks, warns him: "The world is in balance, in Equilibrium. A wizard's power of Changing and of Summoning can shake the balance of the world. . . . It must follow knowledge, and serve need. To light a candle is to cast a shadow" (45). Ged listens but he does not hear. During the next year of study, his hatred for Jasper grows until one night his anger overtakes his wisdom and he responds to the boy's challenges. On the top of Roke Knoll, he uses a spell recalled from Ogion's forbidden books to call the spirit of the Lady Elfarren up from the dead. The earth splits and out leaps the black shadow, who tears at Ged's face and knocks him senseless. As Ogion has before, the Archmage Nemmerle saves Ged, but only at the expense of his own life, for Ged's growing power has loosed a power of unlife, a shadow who can work evil through him. After many months of healing, Ged's face is scarred, his speech slowed, and his spirit badly bent. When he finally returns to his studies, now a year behind his peers, his shame increases his isolation.

On the eve of Ged's seventeenth birthday, Vetch renews their friendship, returning the otak to Ged's care and exchanging true names with him: Vetch becomes Estarriol and now knows the boy Sparrowhawk as Ged. Exchanging true names proves a profound trust, for "who knows a man's name, holds that man's life in his keeping" (69). Estarriol has generously given Ged this sign of his deep faith in him.

Finally, having earned his staff—and thereby become a full-fledged mage—Ged moves to the small village Low Torning, where he begins to mature. The humble village offers neither glory nor fame, but Ged's willingness to serve selflessly without pride earns him the respect of the villagers. Still battling his fear of the unnamed shadow, Ged courageously agrees to approach the Dragon of Pendor, whose nine spawn threaten Low Torning. Using his intellectual knowledge of history and geography, he figures out the true name of the dragon, thereby disempowering it. Later, when tempted by the lovely Serret, Ged recognizes the deceit in her words and uses his will to resist her evil. However, again he uses magic impetuously, transforming himself into a falcon and flying over the Osskil Sea to Gont, escaping "the botched beasts, belonging to ages before bird or dragon or man" (122) and his fear. Again Ogion must rescue him. This wise father figure warns him against using the changing spell again, "losing one's self, playing away the truth" (125). Ogion advises Ged to cease running from his shadow and to pursue it to its source and name it. "You must seek what seeks you. You must hunt the hunter" (128), he advises.

Finally, supported by Vetch, who accompanies him out from the inward sea, Ged finds his shadow. He faces it alone, without magic, and names it as part of himself. Now Ged is a man who, "knowing his whole true self, cannot be used or possessed by any power other than himself" (181).

Le Guin in "The Child and the Shadow" describes how the adolescent feels guilt and repugnance for the self he or she sees as shadows, "warts, and fangs and pimples and claws and all . . . as part of him [or her] self. The ugliest part, but not the weakest. For the shadow is the guide inward and out again. . . . The guide of the journey to self-knowledge, to adulthood, to the light."[4] Critics Craig and Diana Barrow discuss the similarity of the shadowy figure and its influence on Ged's life to the American Indian trickster figure, often identified as Coyote, who represents the useful but often thoughtless or amoral primitive stage of consciousness of untrained infants.[5] Despite the possible destructiveness of these behaviors with regard to social cohesion, these elements of greed, self-centeredness, and spontaneity can be useful and sometimes even attractive, especially when they are nonthreatening to our image of ourselves. The shadow is necessary.

*A Wizard of Earthsea* is the journey of a young creator of magic images from an ignorant and arrogant youth to a skilled artist of power, one humbled by his understanding of the truth that "as a man's real power grows and his knowledge widens, ever the way he can follow grows narrower: until at last he chooses nothing" (71). For Le Guin, maturity comes when a person can sense the equilibrium between seeking only good and avoiding evil, admitting and accepting the imperfect parts of one's self rather than projecting them onto others or pretending they are not there. The mature human realizes the balance of life and unlife and can control his or her actions with courage, yet can also wait passively, wisely attending to the rhythms of the world. Le Guin's understanding of the archetypal image of the journey from impetuous self-centered childhood to mature responsiveness to the beneficial directions of human society as part of the natural world reflects her Taoist principles of including and balancing opposites rather than choosing and avoiding aspects of life.

Le Guin uses the language of fantasy to create a clear and graceful artistic image of this truth; she tries to convey its true name by reaching beyond the reader's intellectual grasp of simple definitions toward the more complex comprehension that comes from experiencing a story imaginatively. As she writes in "Dreams Must Explain Themselves," "Wizardry is artistry. The [Earthsea] trilogy is then, in this sense, about art, . . . about the creative experience" (*Language of the Night,* 53).

*A Wizard of Earthsea* is about the creation of self, a coming of age. Traditionally for males, this means becoming a hero who learns to ride the waves of a world, accepting knowledge when it is needed, and courageously grappling with the darker side to create spaces for light.

## The Tombs of Atuan

Through the use of metaphor, this novel focuses on sex, the traditionally female coming of age, the creative act through which girls break the bonds of their youthful ignorance, are reborn, and become free, not as the intelligent, action-oriented male heroes but as the mysterious, emotion-laden forces of myth and legend. *The Tombs of Atuan,* which won the Newbery Honor Book Citation, is set 15 years after Ged has faced his shadow and accepted his dark side as part of himself. Now a full-fledged hero, he undertakes the mission to obtain the missing half of the ring of Erreth-Akbe from the Tombs of Atuan, which will enable him to restore peace to all of Earthsea. However, this novel begins not with Ged but with a small girl, five-year old Tenar, running through an orchard in the evening, her black hair outlining her tiny white face, the black sky framing the tiny white evening star, as she circles back toward her golden-haired mother. The mother grieves because her youngest daughter will soon leave her to train as a priestess of the Tombs, where the nameless gods of darkness and death take away her name and call her Arha, the "eaten one." The ritual in which she is entombed, put to bed alone with her hair shorn, is similar to American Indian puberty rites (Barrow and Barrow, 25).

Margaret Esmonde notes how this novel parallels classical mythologies of Western culture,[6] but with important differences. Arha's conventlike new home celebrates mystery, death, and ignorance. Unlike the appetizing fruits of Eden or of Greek myth, the apples in the Place of the Tombs are yellow, raised for drying. Penthe, a fellow novice who serves only because her parents were too poor to support her in the outside world, gives Arha eight undried apples, which remind her of her former life among the living. To Bruno Bettelheim in *The Uses of Enchantment,* the apple represents knowledge of love and sex, as in the Biblical garden of Eden and the fairy tale of Snow White.[7] Like the young virginal Snow White, who while serving seven sexless dwarf miners in the dark forest is trapped by a jealous stepmother, Arha is trapped as a novice in an airless, stifling cavern by the high priestess Kossil, who is jealous of Arha's future position as the One Priestess of the Tombs of Atuan. Separated from the male world of adventure and sunshine in the moonlit darkness of underground knowledge, of silence and death, Arha becomes habituated to the solitude and sterility.

As mistress of nine dark tombstones, whose significance she does not understand, she learns to travel in the labyrinth to the Undertomb, which hides a treasure she doesn't even want to see. Because no light is allowed below, she travels the dusty, dangerous corridors by touch, memorizing the count of the turns, following rote directions of the dry, stick-thin priestess, Thar, who teaches her about the Nameless Ones, the ancient masters of dark and death. This priestess is not cruel, but she lives by the "iron law"[8] of her faith. Kossil, the heavy, crafty High Priestess of the Godking, serves not because she believes, but because she covets power; it is she who most obstructs Arha's desire to know more. Arha is protected by the simple eunuch Manan, a warden who has been assigned to protect her from the dangers of too much knowledge and curiosity, but who bends the rules in his love for her. To ensure a life of security, Arha need only obey the rules carefully explained by Thar, avoid threatening Kossil's ambitions, and wallow in the adoration of Manan; in short, she need not accomplish or learn anything new. Le Guin is painting the traditional role of the female acolyte of myth and legend who knows the dark emotional mysteries of the inarticulate subconscious, knows them by touch and by rote rather than intellect or logic. The treasures of the tomb may represent female sexuality, symbolically connected with secrecy, darkness, and death.

Though schooled in faith and fear, Arha becomes curious as she matures. Growing into adolescence, she ventures more deeply into the labyrinth than any before her, fascinated as she realizes her power within this dark realm. Early in her teens, she lets three would-be thieves who are trapped in the labyrinth die, ignoring them as if they were not even human. But at 15, when she spies another intruder—Ged—she takes him food and water; like Rolery in *Planet of Exile,* she is curious to know more about this young man from an outside realm, and she is inexplicably attracted to him. Defying Kossil's power and Manan's concern, she protects Ged from the death they order. When he asks to be taken to the treasure room, not to raid its precious metals and jewels, but to fetch the second half of the ring of Erreth-Akbe, she complies. Arha has known the path to this great treasure but had never before cared to see it: "Some feeling that her will or her knowledge was not yet complete held her back" (46). If this treasure is symbolically equated with her sexuality, she has not been ready before now.

When Ged says her true name, Tenar, calling her to hold on to the living world of her origin, Arha begins to feel that her life in the tomb is empty and futile. Her awakening interest in new life is analogous to a girl's emerging sexual awareness. The scars on Ged's face, tokens of his own experiences with darkness, convince her of his wisdom, for it is darkness that is familiar to her. Fear, darkness, and ancient ritual may be powerful, but humans thrive in light. She trusts him, and lets him trust her; together, they begin the tortuous journey from the dark tombs toward the light, a journey neither could make alone. Now Tenar is reborn into a world where she will learn to speak with many people, to read, to reach out toward all the adventures of freedom. Accustomed to faithful obedience, this new world of choice and learning frightens her. Ged accompanies her only to Re Albi, where she will have to learn her own way to travel, but she faces the new world bravely, knowing she is capable of keeping trust and of trusting.

In Western culture, sexual maturation is difficult, especially for girls, whose first sexual adventure often demands a commitment and a concomitant trust. The sexual awakening of Tenar is not so much a consciousness of physical processes but of the psychological necessity of connecting with other humans by sharing experiences and language. Le Guin captures that adolescent tentativeness about both kinds of connection by describing Tenar's shyness first about actually touching Ged and then her flash of doubt that causes her to raise her knife against him. Ged's mature confidence reassures her. In the end, Ged makes no false promises, allowing Tenar her own future, offering his best gifts of help in times of need and his trust in her abilities to grow. He is an unusually generous hero. Even so, the difference between the exciting adventures of his youth and the dreary prison of Tenar's upbringing is painfully obvious. Le Guin helps the reader experience the sharp contrast between the traditional male heroic activity and the silent passivity of the female protagonist. Yet Tenar is not without power or courage. As the critic Holly Littlefield points out, at 15 years old, with no training in heroism, Tenar rebels against the education that tried to stifle independent thinking and "manages to outwit, entrap, and control the most powerful wizard in the land."[9] Moreover, she enables him to succeed in his mission. However, as Elizabeth Cummins notes, "Le Guin has created a woman and then was unable to imagine an appropriate place for her in the hierarchical, male world she had created" (Cummins, 156). Rather than remain in the city of Havnor, where she will be courted for her beauty and grace, Tenar opts to settle on the tiny island of Gont with Ged's old mentor, Ogion.

## The Farthest Shore

In *The Tombs of Atuan,* Tenar is reborn by wrenching herself out of the secure habit of trying to live within herself. In the next novel in the series, *The Farthest Shore,* which won the National Book Award for Children's Literature, the hero, Prince Arren, is reborn when he resists the security of devoting himself to the search for eternal life. Becoming genuinely aware of the inevitability of death is a "coming of age but in larger context," writes Le Guin, for "the hour when a child realizes . . . that he/she, personally, is mortal, will die, is the hour when childhood ends, and the new life begins" ("Dreams," *Language of the Night,* 55). Just as Tenar has courageously abandoned her familiar land of the dead to seek new knowledge, Arren dares to leave his childhood home for an unknown destiny. When the book begins, the young prince has traveled to Roke to report the lessening of magic in his father's kingdom, the lack of caring about true names and about "looking at the world."[10] Now Archmage, Ged listens and invites Arren to accompany him on a journey to discover why the world has gone awry, a journey directed by the winds and waves of fate.

What has gone awry in the world of Earthsea? Le Guin writes that "wizardry is artistry" (*Language of the Night,* 53) and art is "looking for the outside edge" (28), using the imagination to notice the physical things of the world, paying enough attention to one's inner reactions to discover the connections among emotions, memories, and experiences to learn a fuller reality than what is superficially evident. Magic fades when the will to listen and learn the true names of the things of life pales. The world of Earthsea is going awry because its inhabitants are looking for a false dream outside of life, the dream of eternal security, which is found only by living superficially instead of delving deeply into dangerous exploration and living wholly and passionately as do artists and magicians.

Although Ged is Archmage of Roke, the Isle of the Wise and the center around which all else moves, he can only guide. The King of All the Isles, traditionally seated at Havnor, must rule and keep the peace. The Archmage gives fealty to the king, whom he trusts to follow the pattern of balance as discerned by the mages of Roke. King Maharion, who died 800 years before, had prophesied: "He shall inherit my throne who has crossed the dark land living and come to the far shores of the day" (*Farthest Shore,* 17). Now Ged asks Arren to attempt that journey. He calls Arren the son of Morred, the last great king of Havnor, but Morred had died 2,000 years earlier. Arren is reluctant, for he had hoped to return home with a prompt cure for his father's woes. "It was as if the Archmage had named him son of myth, inheritor of dreams" (20). Ged has won the crown for a king and fetched the lost Rune of Peace from the tombs of Atuan, but the present king, Arren's father, is unable to keep that peace. Le Guin differentiates between the mages, whose power is their sensitivity to truth and wisdom, and the kings, whose rule depends on their ability to convince their people to live by that wisdom.

The Master Patterner, a mage who is especially sensitive to the overall state of Earthsea, explains, "There is a weakening of power. There is a want of resolution" (23). Arren is afraid; he is no mage, no king; he is merely himself, a young boy. But Ged reassures him and urges him to live up to his true name, Lebannen, which signifies the rowan tree, whose roots run deep and needs only time and space to grow. Ged offers him this journey as his destiny, and Arren finally accepts, for he has the sword of

Serriadh, which can only be drawn in the service of life. This sword is the source of his use-name, Arren. He follows, for "now the depths of him were wakened, not by a game or a dream, but by honor, danger, wisdom" (8).

Like the youthful Ged, Arren is impatient to learn and he finds the silence of his mentor irksome. He had expected immediate answers, but Sparrowhawk-Ged only responds with vague answers about the necessity for balancing the equilibrium of the world and avoiding personal actions that would upset that balance: "When we crave power over life—endless wealth, unassailable safety, immortality—then desire becomes greed. And if knowledge allies itself to that greed, then comes evil" (35). What hero wants to hear this? Traditionally, heroes gather courage and knowledge to act, to change the world and attain wealth, safety, and perhaps even immortality for themselves and their people. Le Guin recognizes the difficulty of this slower, humbler patience in following the Taoist way of maintaining balance by acting only when necessary, a philosophy that, because it depends on a sensitivity to rhythms as they unfold rather than on a set of articulated rules and ideals, is necessarily vague and nondirective. "There is a certain bleakness in finding hope where one expected certainty" (36), and Arren fights that bleakness for much of his journey.

The two sail in Ged's boat, *Lookfar*, to Hort Town, a bright, shoddy place full of drug addicts. There Ged finds Hare, a former wizard now addicted to the drug hazia, for which he has given up his true name. Ged tries to follow Hare into his dream to ascertain the source of this evil tendency, but meanwhile Arren, distracted by his own vision of a tiny light promising eternal life, is kidnapped by the pirate Egre. In his youthful arrogance, Arren has shifted his attention from Ged and given in to temptation. Again, Le Guin indicates the dangers of misplaced goals; living on earth is more productive than seeking security in an afterlife.

Ged rescues Arren, and they continue to Lorbanery, which they find equally dimmed. Formerly renowned for their silk weaving, the inhabitants have traded their looms, now covered with spider webs, for the promise of freedom from death. The dyer Sopli, who thinks he knows the place where life is escaping, accompanies Ged and Arren on their journey to the west. So afraid is Sopli of the water that he crouches like a spider in the boat, fearful of the ever-changing sea that leads to death but also to life. Ironically, he drowns himself in this sea, fleeing from the arrows suddenly raining down from a formerly friendly island. Avoiding danger only leads to nonlife, the same kind of fearful existence that led Ged to make perilous mistakes in his youth, as related in *A Wizard of Earthsea.*

Ged is wounded, and Arren, less and less sure of the value of wizardry and magic, sinks into a depression. Feeling as if he were wrapped in cobwebs, and paralyzed by his fear of the death that seems to hang over Ged, he barely expends the effort to keep his mentor alive. The two are rescued by sea-people aboard a raft-colony, an invention that Le Guin had written about in an early unpublished story. These people, "stalk-thin and angular . . . like strange dark herons or cranes" (112) live beyond all the islands, touching land only once a year to repair their rafts and replenish their supplies. Even this easy-going tribe is affected by Earthsea's tragic loss of joy and magic, for they cannot complete the songs of their annual celebration of the Long Dance. However, young Arren, having confessed his fears to Ged, now learns that though reality may seem hollow, void of meaning and joy, "there must be darkness to see the stars. The dance is always danced above the hollow place" (121). Ged explains that we only have "the gift of selfhood" (122); yet, if we would only use that fully, it is enough. The People of the Open Sea live simple lives away from most temptations and wickedness, but "in innocence there is not strength against evil" (124). Now Arren takes courage from Ged and is able to sing through the night for them. For Le Guin, completing journeys and the rituals that mark them is important for keeping in tune with the rhythm of the universe; heroes earn their titles as much for maintaining the order of life's dance as for stopping the dances of others.

Now the dragon, Orm Embar, arrives and asks Ged and Arren to continue their journey to Selidor, where the source of evil seems to be. Here they find Cob, a former mage who had misused his wizardry by frivolously raising the spirits of the dead. Cob, whose name means "spider" (as in cobweb), had greatly feared death. Once, in a fit of anger, Ged had sent him to the land of the dead, and now Cob is avenging that punishment by opening a hole between the world of light and the dark dry land of death. By opening the possibility of even a shadowy life after death, he is draining from Earthsea the magic, the joy of creation, and the will to live fully and passionately. The great dragon Orm Embar sacrifices himself, crushing Cob, who cannot die but is injured enough that he cannot harm Ged. Now Arren and Ged must cross the land of the dead to stop up the hole.

The critic Bucknall compares Le Guin's concept of death to that expressed by poet Rainer Rilke in *Duino Elegies* (1922). Like Rilke, Le Guin believes that consciously acknowledging death's inevitability leads to a fuller, more passionate embrace of life, and its denial means a deathlike life, full of fear and caution. When Arren and Ged reach the hole, Ged expends all of his magic to close this unnatural passage between life and death. Arren must help him return through the lands of the dead to the beach of Selidor, where the oldest dragon, Kalessin, meets them. Having faced death, Arren now lacks fear; he struggles valiantly to save Ged. But the dragon has come not to threaten but to honor their deed and to carry them back to Roke. There, Ged acknowledges Arren, now Lebannen, as the king the land has awaited so long. Then Ged returns to Gont. "He is done with doing" (196). Now he will be.

As a heroic legend, the Earthsea Trilogy is the story of the hero Ged, who learns first to conquer himself and manage his powers through patient wisdom and modesty. Then he rescues his female counterpart, Tenar, from the darkness of passive ignorance and obedience placed upon women by tradition. Finally he acts as the mature master, preparing a new hero while facing the demise of his own youthful strength and power. As a universal myth, the trilogy concerns all humans who strive to live wisely and deeply. Whereas one critic believes the trilogy reflects no overt political or theological stance,[11] the scholar T. A. Shippey writes that by the third volume, "Earthsea begins to resemble America in the aftermath of Vietnam: exhausted, distrustful, uncertain."[12] So perhaps Earthsea is also the story of our Western culture, emerging first from the traditional pride of individual conquest, then recognizing the dangers of ignorance and obedience for women, and finally facing the mortality of Earth and acknowledging that power must be accompanied by humility. Future leaders must learn to listen for the true names behind facile interpretations of history and to respect the creative imaginations of modern mages, who study life's rhythms writ large.

## Tehanu: The Last Book of Earthsea

A recent addition to the trilogy, which changed it to a series, seems the most political, not only in its striking feminism, but in the deep sense of doom that pervades it, a doom felt by many observers to embody the increasing breakdown of peace and order. *Tehanu: The Last Book of Earthsea* was composed 20 years after the trilogy by a different Le Guin, a more experienced woman who wants to balance the heroic-male focus of the earlier books with a novel centered around womanly pursuits. The protagonist, Tenar of the *Tombs of Atuan,* has studied with the mage Ogion but has chosen the freedom to live in the world as a wife and mother on a farm in Gont rather than the isolation that special powers and authority impose. Her new name is Goha. "She was seeking something that Ogion could not give her" (Littlefield, 254): touch, love, the fullness of the ancient power of women. Now an elderly widow, she has taken in a young girl, horridly disfigured by her abusive father. Therru, burnt so badly she can hardly breathe or speak, also seems mentally dull.

When Ogion, near death, sends for his former pupil, Tenar and Therru travel to Re Albi to care for this powerful man as he dies. However, when mages appear a day later to honor the Ogion, they ignore his old friend as she reveals his true name and utterly disregard the child, whom Ogion had prophesied will be a leader of great power. Ged also arrives, too late to attend Ogion. Disheartened by the loss of his magical power and his waning physical strength, Ged remains with the two females, in need of

Tenar's care. She grumbles as she performs the many dirty domestic tasks necessary to keep them all alive, but she teaches both her charges the womanly arts of survival: cooking, animal husbandry, and patience. From this "less-sanitized side of life" (Littlefield, 255), she has learned the compassion that led her to rescue Therru. She also teaches Therru the ancient creation legends, for Ogion, on his deathbed, had advised her to teach the young girl all.

When the powerful mages come again to search for their new leader, guided by the Archmage's last advice, "to look for a woman on Gont," they again fail to heed Tenar's advice, this time to seek the most ancient dragon Kalessin, for Tenar-Goha does not fit the image of power they seek. Tenar's increasing bitterness about human nature is validated by the attempted assaults on her and Therru by men who seek to punish them for their vulnerability, and by the return of her son, who refuses to share in the hard work of maintaining the farm that is his by law. When the small family returns to Re Albi to nurse the elderly witch Aunty Moss on her deathbed, Tenar feels herself grow heavy and stupid. As they approach, they are greeted by someone vaguely familiar, a false mage, who casts a humiliating spell on Tenar and Ged, by which Tenar must crawl, silent and leashed like a mistreated dog, and Ged, helpless, can only lead her. Meanwhile, Therru calls for help in the language she knows without having to learn it—the ancient language of the dragons. Just as the impostor mage is forcing Ged to push Tenar over a cliff, Kalessin, the dragon from *The Farthest Shore,* rescues them. He greets the young girl who summoned him as Tehanu, a fellow member of the eldest race (i.e., dragons).

Therru, unlike the ancient dragons who refuse to learn, has let herself be taught by the woman of Gont, combining the strength of pure instinct with knowledge. She recognizes Kalessin as Segoy, who raised land from the sea in the story Tenar passed on to her from Ogion, and knows eventually she will join the dragons "on the other wind" (240). For now, though, she will stay with Tenar and Ged. The three will settle in the kingdom, still darkened with confusion but now lit slightly by their hope.

What is Kalessin, and what promise does the dragon bring? A clue lies in Ged's explanation to Arren, now King Lebannen of Earthsea: "We men dream dreams, we work magic, we do good, we do evil. The dragons do not dream. They are dreams. They do not work magic: it is their substance, their being. They do not do; they are."[13] Le Guin describes them as "wildness, what is not owned . . . archetypes, mindforms, ways of knowing, not as a rigid mold, but as a vital potentiality, a guide into mystery."[14] In this world so threatened by moral, social, and physical self-destruction, perhaps the dragon recognizes Therru's profound understanding of its true state. A female child, abused and disfigured by fire, traumatized, she is the world, perhaps the ashes from which a new dream will arise. Inarticulate in the political language that contextualizes and excuses such damage, this victim recognizes the primal motivations of humanity that can guide us to survival.

Historically, Earthsea seems to be set in a European civilization of the late medieval period, when common folk, tied to the practical chores of survival, knew intimately the materials and rhythms of the natural world and were more attuned to the intuitive knowledge of myth and legend. Educated modern people know this world in a more abstract way, less acquainted with the visceral physical habits of daily experience, less capable of knowing and naming the true nature of things in the world. In his 1977 review of the Earthsea Trilogy, Dennis O'Brien writes,

> The journey to modernity can be seen as the loss of names, the inability to summon any spirit at the core of the things and events. The old powers are still there, but they are now regarded as nameless and resist being called by name. . . . The strength of Ursula K. Le Guin's writing is to make us feel the spiritual struggle between a world to be summoned and a world of nameless power.[15]

His observation is especially valid for this final volume, which describes most vividly the loss of magical control, the fading of the ability to name.

Clearly a feminist challenge to the traditional heroic adventure, *Tehanu* is bleak and beautiful in its impact, the stammering plot and stuttering characters reflecting the horrible uncertainty of people without power in a terrifying world. Le Guin herself recognized the strength of this work as she was writing it, recording the story without knowing where it was going. "I held my breath, closed both eyes, sure I was falling. . . . I wrote the book outside, even in autumn when the rain dripped off the verandah roof. . . . I didn't want to leave Ged and Tenar and their dragon child safe. I wanted them free" (*Earthsea Revisioned,* 26).

The novel received mixed reviews, praised by some for its spare stark power and damned by others for its "corrosiveness."[16] Some critics questioned whether the book was written for the same young audience as the previous three: "a little too autumnal . . . nearly too shocking for its supposedly young adult pages."[17] "Young readers should be obliged to wait a decade or two before they read it."[18] Yet critic Meredith Tax agrees with Le Guin that the division of literature by intended audience is a false one. The Earthsea books, including *Tehanu,* are "children's literature like the *Odyssey* and *Beowulf* [both common in the public school curriculum] are children's literature . . . , if children are the only ones who need stories that remind us of the firelight flickering on the walls of caves."[19]

To read the Earthsea Cycle is to enter a mythic world where the pattern of time extends beyond human history and knowledge extends beyond human logic. These novels stun the attentive reader with their impact. Though easy to comprehend as adventures, they, like other great myths, are difficult to explain in the traditional thematic, "nonfictional" language of teaching. Le Guin explains more clearly:

> The great fantasies, myths, and tales are indeed like dreams: they speak from the unconscious to the unconscious, in the language of the unconscious—symbol and archetype. Though they use words, they work the way music does: they short-circuit verbal reasoning, and go straight to the thoughts that lie too deep to utter.[20]

# 4. Connecting the Hainish Dance and Collective Power: *The Left Hand of Darkness, The Lathe of Heaven, The Word for World Is Forest,* and *The Dispossessed*

While exploring mythic questions in the Earthsea series, Ursula K. Le Guin was also considering the effects of various political and social formats on the Hainish world. In these later books, she uses the metaphors of science fiction more skillfully than in her first three novels to articulate the problematic nature of basic assumptions about human nature regarding gender, social and ethnic differences, the value of ownership and stockpiling, and the natural world. In addition, Le Guin continues to challenge the way we use language to classify people and to establish priorities for our attention and care. Above all, these next books explore our social relationships by involving the reader in worlds both familiar and new, using rhythm, story, and image to help us more fully participate.

Le Guin prefers a society that governs by consensus, a communal cooperation without "external" government that she calls anarchy. Although small societies of about 2,000, as in *The Eye of the Heron,* are preferable, larger groups could be organized with the help of technology. A computerized, centralized agency could organize the equal distribution of work and resources, allowing citizens to choose their tasks according to their talents and interests except in times of emergency. This is the kind of loose centralization in *The Dispossessed* and in *Always Coming Home.* Le Guin's distaste for hierarchical power structures based on traditional definitions of status is obvious as early as the Hainish science fictions wherein the authority of traditional leaders is undermined by folk knowledge and common sense. She also undercuts the traditionally higher status of light-skinned people by portraying dark-skinned people as socially preferable. Later, as she developed a more feminist consciousness, she began to challenge the traditional attitudes about the roles of women and men. Her ideal women are usually independent and spontaneous, strong enough to question the limitations of the conventional roles in their society, yet sensitive and sympathetic to the feelings of others, including men. Often Le Guin's women express a special fondness for children and an appreciation of both artistic and natural beauty, but then so do her male characters.

With regard to social characteristics, Le Guin seems to prefer peace-loving gentle folk, like the Fians, whose affinity for the natural environment keeps them from aggression. Yet Le Guin resists any one-sided model. Aggression and competition are also natural traits of whole mature beings, the shadowy part that must be recognized and integrated. Pain and anger are unavoidable and sharing them fosters community. The danger of a communal society in which competition is stifled is that individual differences become flattened. Although capitalist societies foster the existence of an economically deprived class, they also provide unlimited time and resources for those few who can stretch intellectual and artistic bounds. The danger of rigid communalism is the dreariness of mediocrity; the advantage is a relatively just distribution of resources to everyone. Le Guin explores the subtle implications of these dynamics in the four novels discussed below.

## The Left Hand of Darkness

By 4870 A.D., when this novel takes place, the League of Worlds embraces 83 planets and has been renamed the Ekumen. Le Guin's father, Alfred Kroeber, used the Greek word for "household," oikoumene, to describe the tendency of cultures to share characteristics as they come in contact with each other (Cummins, 73). Le Guin introduces this concept to her readers along with the frigid setting of *The Left Hand of Darkness* in her short story "Winter's King": "The dream of the Ekumen, then, is . . . to regather all the peoples of all the worlds at one hearth."[1] The ultimate goal of the Ekumen seems to be the development of close loyal relationships across cultural boundaries of race, traditional enmities, and even gender. The dilemma is how to achieve those close bonds without encroaching on an individual's freedom not only to survive but to flourish creatively. *The Left Hand of Darkness* picks up the theme of loyalty across cultural boundaries from the earlier three science fiction novels and expands it into an exploration of gender-based prejudices.

Genly Ai, a Terran envoy of the Ekumen, has been sent to invite the inhabitants of the frozen planet Gethen, also called Winter, to join. Having landed in the Gethen kingdom of Karhide, Genly Ai believes he has made a valuable contact in the prime minister, Estraven. The night before his first audience with the king, however, he becomes uncertain of the first minister's loyalty; Estraven's strange, womanly vagueness, "all charm and tact and lack of substance,"[2] irritates Genly. The next day, he discovers that Estraven has been branded a traitor to Karhide and has fled to the neighboring Orgoreyn. Genly is shocked at Estraven's lack of patriotism. Soon after, discouraged by the Karhidish king's rejection of his invitation to join Ekumen, Genly also goes to Orgoreyn.

While the Karhides had seemed chaotic, more interested in formal courtesy than in practical logic, the Orgorets are technically organized; they ask direct questions and provide physical comfort. After presenting his proposal, Genly thinks he has achieved success, except for a vaguely sensed unease. However, his suspicion seems silly in the face of the genial hospitality shown to him, especially after Estraven, whom he distrusts and dislikes, warns him of Orgoreyn insincerity. Nevertheless, his illogical suspicions prove true. He is suddenly arrested and carted off to Pulefen, a prison where he is drugged and worked to near death, weakened by cold and lack of adequate food.

When all seems lost, the person he least trusts—Estraven—rescues him. Now the only hope for their survival is an 80-day trek across the Gobrin ice sheet to the Karhide border. Together, they accomplish this superhuman feat on skis, learning to trust each other, to understand each other's differences, and to use them to succeed. When Estraven is killed, Genly realizes he has lost a beloved friend, a partner whose loyalty to the same cause he serves—the good of all—transcended the personal and the merely patriotic. Together, the two have accomplished the mission of the Ekumen. Karhide will join and Orgoreyn will follow.

Although the plot centers around the nature of loyalty and betrayal, most readers and critics focus on the issue of gender, which Le Guin herself admits is a central theme.[3] In her critical overview, Bucknall calls this novel Le Guin's first contribution to feminism (Bucknall, 9), and indeed the story raises thought-provoking questions about our tendency to polarize, to divide males and females not only biologically but socially, politically, and psychologically. The Gethenian people are hermaphroditic, biologically becoming either male or female only every 26 days when they are in "kemmer," a short period of sexual readiness similar to times of estrus in animals. Partners automatically change to the opposite of the other, and individuals can both impregnate and conceive during the course of their lives. In 1969, when Le Guin wrote the book, the feminist movement was in its infancy. Her 1976 essay "Is Gender Necessary?" identifies the androgyne as a symbol for the integration of the Taoist yang (the masculine element) with the yin (the feminine element), qualities our culture tends to separate. Traditionally, literary male heroes are active doers, people who accomplish deeds, and female protagonists are passive admirers, keepers of the status quo. Genly Ai finally realizes that he cannot accomplish his mission by mere planning and acting. It needs the readiness of Estraven, who knows the value of submitting to the rhythm of fate, waiting, resting, and watching as well as acting. Qualities traditionally defined as male and female are equally necessary for survival and for inner growth.

In her introduction to the novel, Le Guin calls *The Left Hand of Darkness* a "thought experiment" to explore the implications of a society where there are neither men nor women, but individuals who share the biological and emotional makeup of both. Her results are provocative. On the Gethenian planet, each adult individual shares the "burden and privilege" of childbearing and child care. "Nobody here," Le Guin writes, "is quite so free as a free male anywhere else" (*The Left Hand of Darkness*, 94) but neither is anyone as constricted by work or by cultural limitations. Children don't develop the psychosexual hang-ups identified by Freud, nor is there rape or much seduction. There also is no war on Gethen. Le Guin supposes that a connection exists between two traits considered unique to humans among mammals: their constant sexual readiness and their ability to mobilize forces to wage war. Like other animals on Earth, the Gethenians bicker, quarrel, compete, fight, and even murder on a small scale, but they do not subsume other social needs and resources to an organized military effort. Because Le Guin experiments in the fictional guise of the male envoys sent from Terran, she can depict the chagrin of these former masters whose constant virility is deemed "perverted" and laughable by the Gethenians. She teases male pride gently, a fair-minded proponent of humankind in general rather than a bitter opponent of the male gender.

Besides offering an opportunity for social analysis, the comparison between the male-female gender split on Earth and the androgynous nature of the Gethenians also reflects the differences between the traditional polarization of Western thought and the Taoist sense of unity, represented in the novel by the Karhide philosophy, the Handdarata. Proponents try to achieve insight by "inactivity or noninterference" (60), a trancelike state called an "untrance" by believers, who tend to use negatives to maintain awareness of the shadow side of positive concepts. Answers exist in the chaotic tension between knowing and unknowing, focusing and unfocusing, seeking darkness and shadow as well as clarity and light.

Le Guin repeats the metaphor from the Earthsea series of the spiderlike Weaver, who acts as the focus of the chaotic energy emitted by the foretellers gathered in a trancelike state to answer the questions put to them by seekers. Like science fiction writers, they observe rather than foretell (67), and the Weaver articulates their sense of what is true. In contrast, the Orgoreyn religion emphasizes the positive and the obvious. They seem focused on enlightenment and truth, but by suppressing the shadowy side of truth, they are not wholly honest. The Karhide obsession with "shifgrethor," the face-saving avoidance of direct advice or dis-agreement, misleads and frustrates Genly Ai, but at least it is more honest than the constantly jovial friendliness of the Orgoreyn, who paint everything in a positive way, regardless of truth. The Gethenian translation of "shifgrethor" is "shadow." As in the complementarity of yin and yang, Le Guin insists that enlightenment is only the left side of darkness; both sides are nec-essary for truth.

Le Guin also broadens the definition of fiction in her introduc-tory notes, challenging the separation of art and truth. Novelists use words to describe truths that cannot be reduced to single names or classification, but, like the yin and the yang, are com-prehensible only in the context of a whole, sometimes on an unconscious or unarticulated level. Science fiction is a metaphor to describe social realities without excluding possibilities not yet tried. In the novel itself, Le Guin expands the scope of the tradi-tional linear pattern of the heroic tale with fictional myths, reports, and alternate viewpoints to raise questions about the borders of narrative. There is no objective narrator, for the narra-tor has been invented by the author. Purportedly, the novel's con-tents have been selected by Genly Ai, and so the reader must judge the contents from his perspective: what has he omitted? what motivated his choices? This is simply his version of the story. Genly Ai is a pun on the words for both the egoistic "I" and the seeing "eye" of the human genus (the French *gens*), the general eye of our sexually separated tradition. The main character's vision expands as his relationship with Estraven, especially in the shadowless region of their glacial trip, frees them from their past separateness. There Genly Ai understands the mutual interdependence of loyal friendship, which transcends sexual differences as defined by traditional cultures.

Bucknall explains how the myths and legends between the story chapters expand the theme of incest, introduced as part of Estraven's personal history, to a deeper metaphor for the Karhide political structure and for the growing relationship between him and Genly (12). This structural counterpointing of mythic legendary tales to the central narrative, which at first seem marginally related but universalize and deepen the scope of story and character, is evidence of Le Guin's experimentation with a more inclusive genre of fiction for the "augmentation of the complexity and intensity of intelligent life," in complete faith to the Ekumenical goal she has set for her league of worlds (*The Left Hand of Darkness,* 211). Yet some of the language of this ground-breaking novel seems dated to contemporary readers—including Ursula K. Le Guin—now familiar with nonsexist language:

> Working on the American Playhouse screen adaptation of the book gave me a chance to correct some of the big, fat mistakes I made in the novel. I didn't stretch the language enough to accommodate the idea of a hermaphroditic people. In the book, all the Gethenians are called 'he.' In the screenplay, I got away from that masculine tinge which colors the book. (Commire, 103)

In later works, Le Guin continues to experiment with new ways of using both linguistic and literary forms to prompt readers to become conscious of the implications of equal respect for racial and ethnic differences as well as gender differences.

*The Left Hand of Darkness* is Le Guin's first work of pure science fiction without elements of fantasy. It received much positive attention among critics, winning both the Hugo Award, presented by science fiction fans, and the Nebula Award, selected by writers of science fiction. At the time it was written, Le Guin's ideas about androgyny were new not only to science fiction, but to literature in general. More than 25 years after its publication, this book is still one of her most popular.

## The Lathe of Heaven

This slim volume raises questions about the source and the effects of our dreams, while poking fun at the authority and ethics of psychiatrists. It is the twenty-first century in Portland, Oregon, in a world made dry and dreary by overpopulation and environmental waste. George Orr is tormented by the effectiveness of his dreams, which, since he was 17, tend to come true not only for himself but for the rest of the world as well, causing change with no residual memory, except for Orr.

Orr is like the jellyfish described at the beginning of the book, floating passively along the rhythms of life, in harmony until a rock or a shore appears. Critic Douglas Barbour recognizes Orr as a Taoist sage, a man who has naturally achieved the Taoist goal of passive adjustment to the world and is now horrified at this unwanted power to impose his will.[4] Each of the chapters is headed with a Taoist quotation that emphasizes the thematic focus. The heading for the third chapter is the source of the title: "To let understanding stop at what cannot be understood is a high attainment. Those who cannot do it will be destroyed on the lathe of heaven."[5] Desperately afraid of his dreams and their power to interfere with the world, Orr seeks help first from drugs and then from the psychiatrist Haber.

In contrast to Orr, Dr. Haber is a doer, a dominating Faustian who can barely suppress his impulse to interfere. His blustery, horselike self-pride makes him one of Le Guin's funniest characters. When Haber realizes Orr's power, he cannot resist taking control, using his machine, the Augmentor, to direct Orr's dreams to his own ends. He sees himself as ultimately benevolent, acting for the good of the world, now overcrowded and outworn. When he directs Orr to solve the overpopulation problem, Orr dreams of a plague that wipes out six billion people. Bothered by Haber's use of him, Orr contacts a lawyer, the brisk Heather Le Lelache, a black woman who observes one of their sessions. In this new world made more comfortable for the survivors, he and Heather meet and come to like each other. But Haber grows increasingly ambitious. Heading a Dream Research Institute, he suggests that Orr bring about peace on Earth; the result is an Earth united in fear against invading space Aliens! Horrified, Orr flees to the cabin of his dreams, now made real by Haber, where he tries to avoid more dreaming. Heather finds him there, almost mad from sleeplessness.

Although it is against her nature to play God, she cannot resist trying to set things straight by hypnotically suggesting that Orr dream Haber into an honest, kind man and dream the Aliens off the moon. When Orr awakens, the Aliens have landed on Earth, and Haber is at least honest about his manipulations. Then, when Haber induces Orr to rid the world of racism, and everyone turns battleship gray, Heather is gone, for her blackness is an integral part of her and she cannot exist apart from her racial identity. Finally Haber takes over completely; he instructs Orr to dream that he has stopped dreaming and then hooks himself up to the Augmentor. Haber's horrifying nightmares begin to destroy the world until Orr takes action, struggling mightily through the disaster to turn off the Augmentor, which has emptied Haber's mind forever. With Haber gone, Orr is free to sleep and dream "like the waves of the deep sea far from any shore . . . danc[ing] the dance among all the other waves of the sea" (170) without breaking and changing the shores of Earth. The Aliens turn out to be good, hard-working citizens, a real benefit to Earth. One of them helps Orr find Heather Lelache again in the novel's romantic ending.

*The Lathe of Heaven* is unusual science fiction because its characters seem so ordinary and realistic, and because it uses the metaphor of psychology and dream research instead of the more commonly used technological sciences. The novel was made into a television film produced and directed by David Loxton and Fred Barzyk in 1980 for the Public Broadcasting Service. William C. Dement, a specialist in sleep and dream research Le Guin mentions in the novel, acted as a consultant to the program. The problem-solution shape of the plot mirrors the simplistic polar thinking of many would-be benevolent dictators whose ideas sound sensible but ignore the delicate complexity of our world.

## The Word for World Is Forest

*The Word for World Is Forest* won a Hugo Award after first appearing in *Again, Dangerous Visions,* Volume I, in 1972. Like the equally brief preceding work, *The Lathe of Heaven,* this novel questions the source and ultimate effect of dream states. If something can be imagined, it becomes a possibility, a potential actuality. Le Guin is implying that this is the danger and the power of fiction. The books also share graphic depictions of how destructive misuse of modern technology affects the plants, trees, water, air, and inhabitants of the world. *The Word for World Is Forest* also raises questions about the morality of American involvement in Vietnam. It is an angry book, a tragedy in both tone and in resolution, in sharp contrast to the comic humor and happy ending of *The Lathe of Heaven.*

It is 2368 A.D. and the Terrans from Earth have colonized Athshe, a planet of five heavily forested islands in a warm shallow sea, aptly renamed New Tahiti. "Ocean: forest. That was your choice on New Tahiti. Water and sunlight, or darkness and leaves."[6] The Terrans use this planet mainly as a source of wood, a commodity now scarce on Earth, where the forests have disappeared and the Himalayas have been made into an amusement park. Athshe is inhabited by gentle humanoids reminiscent of the Fians in *Rocannon's World* in both their sweetly vague nature and their communal consciousness. Standing about a meter high and covered by green silky fur, they balance waking worldly interactions with dream states every two hours. They honor their dreams and worship those who can translate them into experience. These forest folk consider the "yumens," who have invaded their planet and are burning their forests, insane, caught up in constant activity and talk, unconscious of the larger, gentler rhythms.

Like Haber in *The Lathe of Heaven,* the colonists have no qualms about interfering. Blind to the virtues of people who are different, they perceive themselves as bearers of a higher order of civilization. The Athsheans live in harmony with the forest, growing orchards, preferring the varied shade of their deeply wooded homes to the harsh glaring sun of the open places cleared by the robosaws of the human loggers. As in other works, Le Guin questions the preference of Western cultures for the metaphor of pure light over the complexity of shadows, which necessitate more careful examination. Perhaps truth is not to be found by vanquishing shadows but by walking among them.

The conflict between these contrasting cultures is told in several chapters from the different viewpoints of the participants. The novel begins with Captain Davidson, an athletic, active hunter, scornful of the dreamy natives and enthusiastically militant about taming this new planet and using its resources to supply Earth. He denigrates these "creechies," many of them now slaves for the human colonists, and has raped the wife of Selver, an Athshean who can link his dreams to his actions, thus changing the direction of his culture. After his wife dies as the result of Davidson's rape, Selver attacks the stronger captain and suffers terrible injuries. He is rescued by the sympathetic Terran Lyubov, but his hate results in a dream of killing. Now the basic nonaggressiveness of his people is radically and permanently changed, for the power of his dreams, like those of George Orr (or any imaginative leader) is that they present newly imagined possibilities for action. For the first time, the Athsheans are capable of murder. They attack the colonists, and people die, including Selver's friend Lyubov. Selver is devastated by the introduction of war into his culture, even though it has saved their lovely wooded land from certain destruction. Davidson, still alive, is exiled to an island completely razed of the trees that might have offered relief from the glaring sunlight or lumber for building a raft to escape; his punishment is ironically appropriate. The remaining Terrans promise never to return, yet the gentle Athsheans are forever changed.

This brief novel is deeply moving and shocking by turns. Because it polarizes good and evil so definitively, it is a simpler book than *The Left Hand of Darkness* and *The Dispossessed*, which balance advantages and disadvantages of diverse cultures and characters and are more typical of Le Guin's complexity.

## The Dispossessed

In a short story entitled "The Ones Who Walk Away from Omelas," first included in *The Wind's Twelve Quarters* and then published separately in 1993, Le Guin retells the myth of the scapegoat as she found it in a William James essay about morality. In that myth, the people in the city Omelas live well, enjoying healthy, happy, lovely lives. However, a single child lives among them in a different state, demented, dirty, hungry, and ignored. The child's existence is no secret; most people of Omelas accept it as a lamentable but necessary condition of their happiness, for to bring the unhappy being into their midst would spoil the beauty and the fun of the present. But a few recognize that ignoring and walking away from the shadowy side—the existence of the poor, the sick, and the uneducated—is wrong. One of those, writes Le Guin, was Odo, the revolutionary leader who left her luxurious life as a respected university scholar on the lush green planet of Urras to begin a new society, using anarchist principles on the planet's barren, arid moon, Anarres.

In *The Dispossessed,* Le Guin explores anarchism fully enough to get beyond the stereotype of the mad-eyed terrorist. In the preface to her short story, "The Day Before the Revolution," she writes that anarchism attracts her because of its ideals of "cooperation (solidarity, mutual aid) and its opposition to any form of authoritarian state,"[7] ideals she finds compatible with her Taoist view of life.

The people on the planet Urras are Cetians, mentioned in *City of Illusions* as the inventors of Terran mathematics and appearing in *The Word for World Is Forest*. Three of Urras's countries are mentioned: A-Io, which has a capitalist society; Thu, which has a socialist authoritarian government; and Benbili, which has a military government that violently represses anarchist elements. Odo, distressed by the split between the luxurious life of the rich and the miserable poverty of the poor, establishes a political philosophy that rejects centralized authority and private property. She establishes a society on Anarres with no explicit government and thus no laws. By the time of *The Dispossessed*, the Odonians have survived on Anarres for seven generations, about 150 years, by sharing equally the scarce resources and difficult work and by prioritizing the welfare of the society over individual desires. A central computerized planning organization in the largest city, Abbenay, assigns work shifts, honoring individual talents and desires as much as possible. Because private property is banned, people take only what they need from storage areas and excess is discouraged. They live in collective domiciles with double rooms and communal dining areas. Trained to avoid egoistic thinking from infancy, the Odonians extend that attitude toward personal relationships. Completely equal, men and women enter into sexual partnerships only by mutual consent. Indeed, the attitude toward sex seems rather permissive, yet public opinion prevents rape or abuse. Children are cared for collectively, though parents are allowed to visit their children whenever circumstances permit. The protagonist of this story is Shevek, a physicist whose brilliance challenges the status quo when his theoretical work sets him apart as more valuable to the community than many of his peers.

Le Guin alternates chapters between Shevek's growing dissatisfaction with the stifling intellectual conformity of his home planet Anarres—culminating in his decision to explore other options on the mother planet—and his even greater disillusionment with the brilliance and comfort of Urras. The novel begins and ends with his journeying between the planets. The chapters ingeniously mimic Shevek's theory, which combines the ability to understand events both in chronological sequence and simultaneously. The theory is a key to developing the ansible—essentially an interplanetary telephone. The first chapter and the ensuing odd-numbered chapters are written in the present tense, recording Shevek's reaction to Urrasti culture, beginning with his departure in a rocket from Anarres. The even-numbered chapters are a chronological history of Shevek's development from a "knobby"[8] baby to a brilliantly inventive physicist whose work threatens the status quo on Anarres. Tall and intense, Shevek has always felt separate or alien, walled apart from his peers by his genius for physics and his earnest idealism. Le Guin based her portrait of Shevek on her childhood memories of Robert Oppenheimer, the renowned physicist, who visited her home and participated in the intellectual discussions there. She gives Shevek Oppenheimer's clear eyes and large ears, as well as his attractive personality, curiosity, and intellectual brilliance (*Language of the Night*, 111).

The book begins with the image of a wall between the landing field of the Urrasti rocket that will transport Shevek from his home planet and the rest of Anarres, a wall low enough to step over but an effective barrier because of the ideological differences it represents. It is more a mental barrier than a physical obstacle. The Anarresti, fearing philosophic contamination, refuse to mingle with the Urrasti who come to trade for the moon's minerals. As Shevek boards the spaceship, he simply steps through a gap, physically mimicking the step he will eventually take in his mind.

As a child, Shevek has often been scolded for egoism by the caregivers in his collective domicile. His father visits him often, but he does not consciously remember his mother, who chose to work elsewhere. Early in his childhood he has a dream in which a dark dank wall holds a keystone, the primal numbers, "both unity and plurality" (33), which dispel the wall and give him great joy. This dream and the magic square (the first nine numbers arranged in a harmonious square with five at the center) are precursors to his mathematical theory. He learns about other walls, especially when he and his friends imitate Urrasti culture by playing a prisoner and guard game and see the effect on a friend they locked up for 30 hours. Shevek is so disgusted he vomits, ashamed of this side of human nature.

The intellectual genius that sets him apart from his peers attracts attention. Sent to the Regional University at Abbenay to work with the renowned physicist Sabul, he begins to realize that not everyone is treated as equally as the Odonian philosophy claims. Shevek is given a single room, and Sabul forbids him to share the Iotic books he has given him to study. Shevek is shocked, for he did not believe knowledge should be privately owned. Even worse, he discovers later that Sabul is stealing credit for Shevek's work.

Shevek's loneliness is assuaged by a brief homosexual affair with his old friend Bedap and then by a more permanent relationship with Takver, a spirited, intelligent young woman who works as a fish geneticist. They become life partners and give birth to their first daughter, Sadik. When a drought strikes Anarres, Takver and Shevek are given labor assignments too distant for them to meet for four long years. Like good Odonians, they willingly participate in this necessary work, but Shevek begins to chafe under the increasing authoritarian elements on Anarres that squelch new ideas and critical commentary. Lacking an overt centralized government, people still obey the force of public opinion manipulated by the central organizing bureaucracy.

Encouraged by Takver, Shevek founds a Syndicate of Initiative to guard against these infringements on Odo's original ideas. The opposition to dispensing his theories subverts the ideal Shevek holds most dear; he yearns to share his own knowledge with the Urrasti, who he feels could help him develop his theory to the point where it could benefit both worlds. The Syndicate helps him surmount the Anarresti wall of defense against sharing different ideas and differing cultures. Using the same philosophical legalism that was used against him, he sways public opinion to support his trip to Urras, a society he perceives as more generous to new ideas. At this point, the retrospective story of his Anarres life (the even-numbered chapters) ends, and the present-tense adventure begins, bringing us back to the novel's opening scene and the quest for reunion with Urras (the odd-numbered chapters): Shevek steps over the gap in the wall surrounding the rocket ship and leaves the moon for its planet.

Life on Urras seems luxurious and comfortable. Shevek is amazed at the gorgeous clothes, the plentiful delicious food, and the intricate buildings. But he is also slightly disgusted. "Excess is excrement" (98), Odo has said, and Shevek's senses are soon cloyed. Accustomed to the equality on Anarresti, he fails to understand the dearth of woman scientists or the submissive behavior of servants. But he enjoys the freedom to work and the intellectual stimulus of fellow scholars. His students are attentive and flattering. However, when he asks certain questions, he is walled in from learning by the "charm, courtesy and indifference" (80) of his hosts. Furthermore, one of his peers confirms his suspicion that the Iotis want him to develop his General Temporal Theory of simultaneity so they can increase their interplanetary power. Perhaps he is being provided with the time and the freedom to develop his theory, but his ideas belong to the powerful faction, who will use them to profit themselves. He is being bought.

Frustrated and morally repelled by the growing evidence of Urrasti violence and greed, and discouraged by the slowness of his work, he escapes for a day with Vea, the flirtatious sister of a colleague. The combination of Vea's seductive dress and alcoholic beverages, both unfamiliar to the Anarresti, causes Shevek to lose control of himself. The next day he experiences an overwhelming shame, a feeling he has rarely felt since he and his childhood friends played prison, but again Shevek's suffering becomes a means of inner growth. In an extraordinary burst of effort, Shevek finishes the work on his theory but is now unwilling to give it to the Iotis. With the help of his servant Efor, he makes his way to the slums of Nio Esseia, a nearby city, where he discovers the shadowy side of this society whose wealth is made possible by the poverty of an underclass. Wanting to help, he offers to speak at a rally as a means of moving through other walls, but the demonstration turns into a riot as police attack in helicopters. Finally, Shevek finds a passage home to Anarres, and on the way gives his ideas to the peace-loving Hainish, who will use them to make communication possible among all the planets.

At home with Takver, he seeks and finds a door through the ideological walls that separate the planetary cultures. Now mature, he and his friends are aware of the shadowy side of Anarres—the limits on their avowed freedoms—and also the enlightened side of Urras. The last chapter is the hinge that joins Shevek's past on Anarres with his present mission on Urras, as he completes his own personal circular journey and simultaneously makes possible more circular journeys of the future. He comes home empty-handed, just as he left, having taken nothing material from either planet, an Odonian "beggarman" to the core.

The first time they meet, Takver and Shevek participate in an argument about the reality of life. Shevek asserts that pain and suffering are the true condition of life, but brotherly love is one way through that pain: "perhaps it begins in shared pain" (62). Odo has left a life of luxury on Urras (or Omelas) because pain was not shared but designated to an underclass. The Odonians choose Anarres's barren landscape and the severe disciplines necessary for original survival, and their sense of brotherhood is much stronger than that on Urras. But, Le Guin seems to ask, is all this pain and sacrifice still necessary? Must the Odonians maintain their isolation from the luxuries available on Urras? Shevek's mother abandoned him for her work and then, caught up in the routine, failed to contact him or his father. Was that pain necessary or even beneficial? The novel's subtitle identifies this as "an ambiguous utopia," and Le Guin poses profound questions about the virtues of anarchy as well as the problems with authoritarian governments. She depicts Shevek and Takver as preferring privacy, art, and individual development to pain when their pleasures cause no pain to others. Sharing pain as equitably as possible dissipates it so it becomes bearable.

The evolving nature of this anarchy is another ambiguous aspect, and perhaps the events of *The Dispossessed* will begin another stage in Anarres. In "The Ones Who Walk Away from Omelas," mentioned at the beginning of this section, Le Guin describes the happiness in Omelas as a balance between sacrifice and appreciation: "Happiness is based on a just discrimination of what is necessary, what is neither necessary or instructive, and what is destructive."[9] The middle category could equal "comfort, luxury, and exuberance," and would be what Shevek appreciates about the Hainish spaceship, the *Davenant,* that transports him back to Anarres: "Its style had neither the opulence of Urras nor the austerity of Anarres, but struck a balance" (*The Dispossessed,* 380). This balance is made possible through the equal sharing of necessary pain and the avoidance of pain for its own sake, which is possible on an ambiguous utopia. In *The Dispossessed,* Le Guin is carrying us through a journey to inspect and experience the possible futures of our world, so that we might become mindful about our choices now.

Although *The Dispossessed* is often categorized as science fiction and reviewed as such,[9] it is also a political analysis, a romance, and an achingly accurate tale of a lonely individual searching to break the walls between himself and others. Often cited with *The Left Hand of Darkness* as a masterpiece of science fiction and as accessible to general readers, *The Dispossessed* has won high acclaim. In 1974 the novel won the American Library Association's Best Young Adult Book citation, and in 1975 the Hugo, the Nebula, and the Jupiter Awards for best novel as well as the Jules Verne Award. Le Guin enjoyed writing one of the first utopian novels about anarchy and one of the few utopian stories written by women. Even so, her protagonist is male; she has written that, until the revival of the feminist movement in the 1970s, she could not easily write in a woman's voice.

After *The Dispossessed,* Le Guin's novels change direction for a while, veering from the metaphor of outer space toward more earthly contexts, though she retains many elements of traditional science fiction in her short speculative fiction. However, she continues to examine political relationships as a major theme. The most recent novel of the Earthsea series, *Tehanu,* centers around the inequity of public power for men and women, and *Always Going Home* is about another utopia, as well as an exploration of the way people learn about each other. Her frequent book reviews for the *New York Times* and other publications often focus on the political implications of continued pollution of the natural environment by powerful industry.[10] Many of her speeches and essays, collected in *Dancing at the Edge of the World* (1989), center around feminist issues of power and language. Thus, Le Guin uses her art to respond to the political situations of our current civilization, although her stories may be set in other centuries.

# 5. Orsinia and Other Far Away Places: *The Wind's Twelve Quarters, Orsinian Tales, The Eye of the Heron, Malafrena, Very Far Away from Anywhere Else, The Beginning Place, The Rose Compass,* and Stories for Children

Although first renowned for her science fiction and fantasy writing, Le Guin also uses her academic background in European culture to explore the tensions between public and personal responsibilities. Beginning with short stories that raise questions about the usefulness of certain commitments and ideas, Le Guin then depicts the turmoil wrought in individual lives by political conflict, especially when one faction wants absolute control over other lives. Finally, in two love stories, she describes the poignant struggles between the fears that keep people separate and the desire to trust another individual deeply.

## *The Wind's Twelve Quarters*

Although all of the stories in the first published collection of Le Guin's short fiction contain elements of fantasy and science fiction, her knowledge of traditional history and literature provides a realistic structure for the surprises of her ideas. The stories are arranged in the order in which Le Guin wrote them, so, to some extent, they act as a retrospective record of her development as a writer and thinker, especially because her introductions identify how each connects to her other work. "Semley's Necklace" introduces *Rocannon's World;* "The Word of Unbinding" and "The Rule of Names" explore the magical power of language of the Earthsea series; and "Winter's King" sets the scene for *The Left Hand of Darkness.* "The Ones Who Walk Away from Omelas" explains and precedes the establishment of the utopian experiment in *The Dispossessed,* whereas "The Day Before the Revolution," celebrates the life of Odo, who has survived to see younger leaders maintain her dream. "Vaster Than Empires and More Slow"—a Le Guin classic—unites the action with the psyche; misfit Porlock finally finds a sympathetic friend in the vegetation of another planet, a biosphere that responds to the emotions of the human animals who visit. "April in Paris," the first fantasy story Le Guin sold, combines the science fiction device of time travel with Le Guin's knowledge of French history and literature, as well as her wry humor. This melange of stories, which displays the wide range of Le Guin's talents and ethical concerns, serves as an excellent introduction to this writer and illustrates her ability to move through the centuries with ease as she plays with our usual view of reality by twisting her kaleidoscope. Europe is a setting as familiar to her as Earthsea or the Hainish universe and provides insights just as strikingly new.

Orsinia, her first major invented country, is obviously central European. The references to Prague; Napoleon; the Austro-Hungarian Empire; and other historical people, places, and events add a tone of authenticity to Le Guin's close analyses of the impact of political involvement on individual lives. She explores this issue in her collection of short stories *Orsinian Tales* (1976) and in the novel *Malafrena* (1979).

## Orsinian Tales

The name Orsinia, modeled on Le Guin's own first name, was created by her in 1951 before she had published any major work. This collection of 11 short stories spans the history of a mythical European country from about 1150 to 1960; each tale ends with a date and a historical place name. "The Barrow," dated 1150 and set near Lake Malafrena, the idyllic mountain village of the later novel, tells how a young count, nominally a Christian, pays homage to the ancient traditions of mountain folk when a self-righteous visiting priest fails to alleviate the pains of his young wife in the throes of childbirth. Only after the priest is sacrificed is the child born; ironically the count's name is later celebrated in the annals of the Christian church. "The Lady of Moge," dated 1640, gently mocks the idealism of the romantic and heroic traditions. "An Die Musik," dated 1938, and incidentally Le Guin's first published story, underlines the irrelevancy of art to the practical human institutions of state, church, or business; its only use is to teach humankind to rejoice.

Critic James Bittner points out that Le Guin emphasizes the circular shape of her journey through time by placing "Imaginary Countries," the chronologically central tale, at the end of the book (93). It describes a family packing up after a summer vacation in which they have based their games and play-names on Norse myths. The professorial father, the affectionate and strong-minded mother, and the three imaginative children are reminiscent of Le Guin's descriptions of her own childhood summers. The tale sums up elements central to the whole collection: an appreciation of the power of the folk wisdom of European culture coupled with a recognition of the pretentiousness of some of its institutions, and the impulse to use this appreciation for the basis of an imaginative world that satisfies yearnings for traditional values yet allows the freedom to invent new pathways. In these stories Le Guin provides insights into her European heritage at different points of time, as well as raises questions about the authority of different traditions: what is true and important about the interplay between individual personalities and institutional authority, and how does it affect our current thinking?

Like most of Le Guin's writing, *Orsinian Tales* pries open traditional assumptions about some basic sociopolitical issues; her writing challenges certainty about what is useful or morally right. When leaders who are certain about their rights refuse to consider other options or to share authority over resources, tragic conflicts often result, both personal and public. Le Guin vividly depicts the struggle between people who choose peaceful complexity and those who would control their lives in *The Eye of the Heron* and *Malafrena*.

## *The Eye of the Heron*

Strictly speaking, *The Eye of the Heron* (1978) is science fiction because of the invented flora and fauna Le Guin uses to capture the ephemeral loveliness of the pacifist ideal in the hands of a militant society and because the setting is another planet. The book opens with a portrait of a wotsit sitting in the palms of the hero Lev; this toadlike creature with mothlike wings changes its color and shape with entertaining speed—fragile, elusive, yet too enchanting to destroy. Like the dancing herons, the wotsit symbolizes continual renewal and hope for a life of gentleness and peace, the quiet that arises from the balanced center between action and inaction. The other fantastic element in this book is the ringtree, a species that initiates the botanical cycle of the red-leafed forests when a single tree explodes its seeds with a loud bang, about once every 10 years. The seeds grow in a circle around the original tree, exploding in turn and creating new overlapping circles. This pattern is the thematic image of the book, which describes two circles of people, each centered on a charismatic leader, whose overlapping is signaled by an explosion. Except for these symbolic elements, the novel realistically presents the traditional struggle between pacifism and authoritarian desire for conquest and power. In her excellent discussion of this novel's imagery, Spivack observes that women occupy the center of this story (112–113). Although the moral and political leaders at the beginning of the book are men, after the fighting has turned their theoretical differences into a power struggle that neither side can win, the women provide the energy and direction for a workable solution. Bucknall points out the similarity between the choices available for Luz, the female hero of this book, and Rolery of *Planet of Exile* (145). Both leave families where they have no power and enter relationships with men who let them grow. While neither participates in the actual battle, both use their minds to promote social change. Perhaps this novel signals a beginning step in Le Guin's path to feminism.

The novel is situated on the planet Victoria, to which the government of Brasil-America had sent a few thousand criminals about a century earlier to establish a penal colony, now a city ruled by the dictatorial boss Falco. Half a century after the initial settlement, 2,000 more people came to Victoria, evicted from Earth not because of their violent criminal nature, but because they refused to participate in the military. These People of Peace establish a democratic agrarian community, named Shantih, near the original city. Until recently the two communities have lived in economic harmony, though the urbane Victorians scorn the nonconfrontational nature of the people they call the "shanty-town" inhabitants. Now, as the population increases and resources become stretched, the People of Peace seek another place to settle, away from the city and its citizens, who increasingly take advantage of their compliance by demanding more work and resources.

As mentioned above, the leader of the city of Victoria is Boss Falco, whose ideal is to establish a nation of rich estates where selected men would be masters of forced laborers from the People of Peace. He would like to recapture the aristocratic life he associates with the Old World of Earth. Part of his fantasy of power is that his daughter Luz will marry a wealthy landowner and produce heirs in the old European tradition. Luz, however, feels trapped by his expectations and by the ladylike manners that keep her from running free like the Shantih women she sees in school.

Like most dictators, Falco uses ignorance to maintain his authority over the people, including his daughter. Although Luz has been sent to school to learn the rudimentary skills of reading, her father discourages her curiosity and active pursuit of knowledge as unladylike and unnecessary. Le Guin's humor emerges with Luz's discovery of the truth that belies her father's aristocratic pretensions from a Red Cross first-aid manual, which had been presented to the colony of prisoners who are her ancestors. This revelation confirms her doubts about the ethical wisdom of her father's choices, especially his desire that she marry his right-hand man, the power-hungry Herman Macmilan.

Luz learns more about an alternative way of life when Vera Adelson, the middle-aged spokeswoman of the People of Peace, is kidnapped by Falco and put under house arrest in his home. Vera resembles the older women made wise by experience described in Le Guin's essay "The Space Crone" (*Dancing at the Edge,* 3–6). She challenges Luz's assumption that men should take political control of the state while women maintain a home for their comfort and raise children for their armies. She explains that men like her father are not as strong or free as they seem but are trapped as much as the people they seem to control by the hierarchic master-servant structures they establish.

Falco traps himself further as he grooms the unscrupulous and arrogant young Macmilan to be his henchman, asking him to raise an army to keep the people of Shantih from settling elsewhere. He would prefer not to lose control over these peaceful farmers and their work. When he and Macmilan plan to invade Shantih, Luz slips away and offers herself as hostage to be exchanged for Vera, who has impressed her with her serenity and independence. In Shantih, she learns more from their young leader, Lev, about their tenets of solving differences through arbitration, noncooperation, and civil disobedience. Lev is convinced that these tactics will work against Falco and his troops and amasses a throng of people. Falco almost agrees to a peaceful solution when Lev and his throng confront the army, but the power-hungry Macmilan suddenly shoots Lev and violence breaks out. Seventeen from Shantih are killed, and eight from the City. In anger, Falco kills Macmilan. Shocked by these results, Luz remains with the People of Peace and convinces them not just to rely on reason but to act on their own behalf. A party sets out into the wilderness to establish a new settlement. There they find a wotsit, the image of the freedom to change that Luz has found, and a heron, the image of the serene strength of peacefulness. A new seed from the ringtree has sprouted.

Originally published as a single long piece in *Millennial Women,* a collection of stories edited by Virginia Kidd,[1] this lovely novel explores the same tension between an egoistic competitive hierarchy and a communal society of shared power as that depicted in *The Dispossessed,* and also the same ambiguities. The aristocratic society can breed elegance, honor, and loyalty as well as injustice, whereas more socialistic or anarchic systems can foster arrogant idealism and wrongheaded waste of resources. Le Guin is too wise to depict one system as perfect. There are other similarities in the novels. Like Odo, Vera has forsaken marriage and childbearing in order to work toward building a better society. Also like Odo, she lives long enough to understand the costs of her heroism; living in Falco's house, where she sees the bonds between father and daughter, Vera recognizes the depth of her own sacrifice. In her next novel, Le Guin expands this theme of the struggle between personal bonds and idealistic sacrifice.

## *Malafrena*

This long historical novel returns to the setting of Orsinia. The time period echoes European history between 1820 and 1830, when reactionary governments tried to reimpose their authority after the revolutionary period of the late eighteenth century. The story centers around the mountainous country estate of Val Malafrena and the fictional capital city Krasnoy, which also appeared in *Orsinian Tales.* Itale Sorde is a university student caught up in vague radical political rhetoric, using abstract phrases of the French and American revolutions without thinking out their impact on the daily life of most people, who survive unaided by family wealth. The Sordes are hard-working landed

gentry; the landscape is spacious, the servants content, and relationships with other families kindly and gracious. Le Guin here
paints a more sympathetic picture of the aristocratic life she challenged in previous novels. This gentry does not seek to control
and exploit others, but rather serves as the managing center of a
society that shares resources. Here the gentry works as hard as
the other workers to maintain a comfortable life.

As in *The Dispossessed,* the chapters of this novel alternate
between personal struggles at home and political unrest in a land
far away, in this case, the city Krasnoy. Itale, incited by French
Revolutionary writers whom he discusses with his adoring sister,
Laura, leaves home for the city to find a new life but also to serve
"the people." He seeks freedom and a purpose. His father Guide,
remembering his own choice to devote his life to the family estate,
refuses to support him financially. Before Itale leaves, he gives
Piera, his childhood friend and the only daughter of Count Orlant,
a copy of *Vita Nuova,* the new life, but she finds it too abstract to
read. She is more interested in the daily particulars of her home,
more appreciative of the personal needs of her elderly friends and
relatives. In Krasnoy, Itale is soon caught up in editing a radical
press and enjoying the social life of the aristocratic Paludeskar
family, especially their daughter Luisa, who is attracted to his
simple country manners and has an affair with him. Political
events come to a head when Itale is arrested for threatening the
public peace and sentenced to five years in prison. Luisa devotes
her considerable energies and influence to arranging his escape,
but horrified at the shell of a man who emerges after two years in
prison, she breaks off their relationship immediately. Itale returns
to the city, just in time to participate in an insurrection of the people against the government. Le Guin's description captures the
exciting first volleys of the battle, the ensuing confusion, and then
the realization that nobody wins in war. The deaths and injuries
of individual friends are more permanent than the slogans and
promises that start it all. Banned from the city, Itale and his
friend Givan Koste flee to Malafrena, where they are welcomed
with open arms and allowed to rest in the comforts of this haven.
Yet Itale knows he will leave again. He has just begun, and life is a

series of beginnings. Le Guin paints an exciting mural of a European youth who leaves home to learn, to expand his mind and spirit, yet finds his power curtailed by traditional politics and the organized military of the urban aristocracy. The journey he must make outward from home and back again is mirrored by the final jaunt in his beloved sailboat, the *Falkone*.

While he has been gone, his sister has developed into an individual strong and wise enough to maintain their estate profitably. Itale is not the only hero of this novel, which also celebrates the courage and skill of a woman who stays home, resists the traditional security of marriage, and forges a life just as new as the abstractions broadcast and defended by Itale. Like *Tehanu*, *Malafrena* illustrates and justifies the worth of domestic work, especially when it provides a necessary harbor for more public political voices.

In the next two novels, Le Guin turns to personal relations. The first traces the shy dance of two middle-class young people who work out a loving relationship that allows each the freedom to develop individually. The second describes the agonizing journey inward for two individuals whose families have not provided the security of a healthy childhood and who must conquer their mistrusts before they can unite as healthy, whole people.

## *Very Far Away from Anywhere Else*

This short realistic novel is a love story for young people told from the point of view of Owen Griffiths, a 17-year-old "intellectual" in his senior year of high school. He explains that when "kids begin to turn into people and find that they are alone,"[2] they begin to panic and join groups to stay invisible. Although he tries to conform, the effort to hide his real feelings makes him feel guilty and then resentful of his guilt. On his seventeenth birthday, his father buys him a car he doesn't really want. Moreover, his mother expects him to attend a nearby state university despite his desire to go to MIT in Boston, where he can study scientific psychology.

When he meets Natalie Field, her self-possession charms him. Although absorbed with her own musical ambitions, she listens to who he really is and accepts him with all his awkward faults. They become fond friends. However, Owen recognizes this relationship as a way to win status with his peers, to appear more "normal," which is the teenager's way of maintaining a protective cloak of invisibility. When he tries to kiss her, expecting that "normal" relationships include sex, she refuses his advances. Distraught, he wrecks his car and sinks into a funk. His grades slip and he ignores his acceptance letter into MIT and their offer of a full scholarship.

Fortunately, when he attends a recital of Natalie's musical version of an Emily Brontë poem, the two renew their friendship. Natalie explains that Hugh's physical advances had come too soon in their relationship, before she had learned the necessary trust for real affection. He had felt rejected as a whole person, instead of understanding her hesitation about sex. Now she helps him find the courage to face his parents and work out a way to develop his individual strengths.

This brief lyrical novel ends happily, as Owen realizes that his love for Natalie will survive without the commitment of sex. She speaks to him through her music just as he speaks to her in words. They recognize the value of their unique relationship, very far away from anywhere else, where each dares to be alone and different because each can reach out and speak to the other. The next novel traces a more painful journey from isolation, with a more treacherous beginning place, toward a more necessary partnership.

## The Beginning Place

Twenty-year-old Hugh Rogers lives a bleak, dreary life as a grocery checker in a trash-strewn, cement-gray, traffic-streaked suburb, where though the streets are named for trees and scenic vistas, the sun glares hot and mean. Except for a fellow worker, an older woman with a wiseacre mouth, few people pay him any attention. Hugh feels trapped, living with an inadequate mother who nags about both his presence and his absences and working at a dead-end job where his mind is filled with prices and his needs eat up the salary he would rather save for library school. Desperately burdened and miserable, Hugh is drawn toward a nearby glade, where the dark cool stream refreshes and calms him. That it is a time and place outside of ordinary consciousness becomes obvious as Hugh notices his watch hardly moves, no matter how long he stays, and it is always twilight. Just as he grows comfortable in this hideaway, he is confronted by an angry young woman who resents his presence in the place she has claimed as her own.

For several years, Irene has followed this path to Tembreabrezi, a fairy-tale village where the inhabitants welcome her to a home more loving and less threatening than her house in the "real" world, where she is abused by her stepfather. This mountain town is cozy in an Eastern European way, the food redolent of cabbage and onions, and the clothes, manners, and language distinctly Orsinian. Recently, however, the peasants seem increasingly impoverished and mysteriously endangered. The leader, Lord Horn, suggests that Hugh, whom Irene resents so fiercely for intruding, could provide the new strength they need for the shadowy errand that might save this starving village.

The motivations and needs of these villagers are only vaguely expressed, since Irene must translate their language for Hugh and she understands it imperfectly. Irene is attracted to the man she calls "Master," a slight dark person like herself, until she perceives his dishonesty and fearfulness, traits she has just discovered in herself. Hugh declares his love to Allia, who is his mirror image. In this place of alternate reality, perhaps another stage of consciousness, the two are learning to recognize and accept themselves. Irene comes to terms with the harsh-appearing authoritarian masculinity in herself that experience with abusive men has taught her to fear. Hugh's attraction to the gentle Allia, who yields easily to the suggestions of others and who looks to others for protection, is a sign that he accepts that feminine part of himself.

Although Irene still resents the need for Hugh, the master declares "You come to speak our word, he to serve our need; this is as it is to be. One and other, other and one."[3] Critic Bucknall suggests that although Le Guin's characters use their "creative imagination constructively, to find a deeper and more satisfying reality, not to escape from reality altogether" (148), they need each other to effect this escape. Irene translates for Hugh and herself, and he provides courage for both to overcome their fears. The starving villagers may represent the waning ability of each individual to continue developing into adulthood; by agreeing to join the mission to save the "villagers," Irene and Hugh unite in a venture to solve their individual problems, and each other's. They set off on the path away from the gate toward the top of the mountain, Irene showing the way and Hugh carrying the sword that will protect them.

As they climb into the cold, they meet a huge fleshy monster, white and disgustingly wrinkled, who like Hugh's mother whines for sympathy and like Irene's stepfather wants to devour the young people. After initially running away, Hugh stabs the huge pulsing belly, killing the symbolic, suffocating dragon that Irene sees as female and Hugh regards as male. Perhaps, because of the unhappy examples of their parents, both Hugh and Irene fear their own sexuality. Together, and in this place away from what is depressing and familiar, they can meet and conquer their dread of mature adulthood. Hugh lies beneath the gross body, injured yet alive. Irene helps him back to the world outside of Tembreabrezi, and having moved beyond the monsters of their pasts, they make tender love. Back in the modern world, a kindly passerby takes them to a hospital where Hugh is cured of his injuries and the two plan a life together, both free to become whole selves.

The portrait of Hugh's life before his escape is deadening: the ratlike routine of his job, the whining insistence of his fearful mother that he remain home when not working, his faded hope that he will ever attain his dream of going to library school. Irene's misery is just as heartbreaking, as she recognizes that for women like her mother who depend on the romantic myths of the popular media, "all the glory can happen and be done with by the age of twenty-two, and one can live for twenty, thirty, fifty years after that . . . without desire" (*The Beginning Place,* 102). The weight, fear, and desperate hopelessness of these young people make their gradual escape into another dimension of reality suspenseful. Will Irene learn to share the haven of Tembreabrezi with Hugh? What threatens this vague, oddly old-fashioned society of peasants? Can the two overcome their antipathy toward each other and find the courage to seek and fight the enemy? These questions move the plot quickly. The reader cannot help but care about these two young people who must struggle so as to drag themselves from their hopeless lives through the gate into fantasy, then fight so doggedly to emerge injured but healed enough to begin a healthy life together.

The magic realism style of this novel is reminiscent of the mixture of real and fantastic details by South American writer Jorge Luis Borges, whose poem "Heraclito" about that time between waking and dreaming is the source of this book's epigraph, "What river is it that the Ganges flows through?" Where do people gain the understanding and courage to survive and overcome the isolating experiences of childhood? Critic Andrew Gordon admires the "characteristic purity and clarity"[4] of this lyrical work that allows the story to answer this question by its existence rather than in explanatory terms.

## The Compass Rose

This collection of short stories seems to mark a turning point in Le Guin's writing, perhaps because it precedes her explorations into feminist thought and psychology, which broadened her definitions of truth and power. Scholar E. F. Bleiler suggests that Le Guin was losing her faith in fantasy as an adequate substitute for reality and was responding with parody.[5] These stories retain the distance from ordinary people and settings of her early work, as well as present an intellectual purity that differentiates them from her later work. Because deep changes in thinking happen over time and emerge into consciousness only gradually, Le Guin's writing reflects her growth in uneven stages. In her introduction to this collection, she acknowledges a center from which other thoughts arise: the nadir, which contains "The New Atlantis," "The Author of the Acacia Seeds," and "Schrödinger's Cat," all of which explore the connection between beginnings and endings. North is the direction toward Orsinia and west toward the approach of death.

"The Diary of the Rose," like *The Lathe of Heaven,* examines the power of a psychiatrist over a patient, this time from the viewpoint of the doctor. The relatively cynical tone of many of these 20 stories is unsettling, perhaps because they proffer so little hope.

## Children's Books

Le Guin uses similar mixtures of fantasy and real life and a much greater dose of humor and hope in her illustrated books published for children. She has insisted that the difference between literature for children and for adults is minimal and that imaginative literature is valuable for all ages: "Fantasy is true, of course. It isn't factual, but it is true. . . . [I]ts truth challenges, even threatens, all that is false, all that is phony, unnecessary, and trivial in the life they [scoffers] have let themselves be forced into living."[6] These stories, bought and read by adults as well as children, often embody psychological realism in imaginative settings that make them accessible to all ages. "Maturity," Le Guin says, "is not an outgrowing, but a growing up: . . . an adult is not a dead child, but a child who survived. I believe that all the best faculties of a mature being exist in the child" ("Why Are Americans Afraid of Dragons," 44).

*Leese Webster* (1979) is about an artistic spider who, alone and lonely in a castle long abandoned by its former inhabitants, whiles away the time by weaving beautiful designs into her webs. However, she feels they lack luster, and they don't provide much sustenance. One day, cleaners come in and, appreciating Leese's art though not the artist, frame her lovely designs behind glass but remove her from the premises, sweeping her out the window. Hungry, afraid, and now outside, Leese makes the best of her situation by doing what she does best—weaving. The next day she is delighted to find that even her plainest designs are bejeweled with dew, as gorgeous as the palace jewels and infinitely more rewarding in a practical way; they draw flies. James Brunsman's illustrations add wit and warmth to this ingenious parable about artists' growth, especially in relation to "abandoned castles" and to the environment.

Other books published for children are *Solomon Leviathan's Nine Hundred Thirty-First Trip Around the World* (1976, 1983, 1988), a global adventure, and *The Adventures of Cobbler's Rune* (1982) and *Adventure in Kroy* (1982). *Fire and Stone* (1989), illustrated by Laura Marshall, is an allegorical creation story about a mountain with a sense of humor. Fearing the attack of an irritable flying dragon, the townspeople jump into Rocky Pond, except for two children and some cats (who don't like to get wet). The children, Min and Podo, feed the dragon the rocks it craves until, satisfied, it falls asleep and becomes what it ate, a large stony mountain. The allegorical theme of the narrative is nicely summed up in a poem, helping young readers understand the connections between the language of fantasy, myth, and fact.

Dedicated to Le Guin's granddaughter Lyra Sofia, *A Ride on the Red Mare's Back* (1992) is a charming story, inspired by the little red-painted wooden Dalarna horse given to Le Guin on a trip to Sweden. These traditional decorative toys, first made by furniture builders from the province of Dalarna, symbolize Sweden to many travelers but lack a particular story, so Le Guin decided to write one for her granddaughter, who loves horses. In the cold North winter, a young girl's father returns home without her brother, who has been kidnapped by trolls. The young girl slips out of the house to look for him, taking with her the red scarf she is knitting and her little red horse. When she meets the first troll, her toy horse turns into a large steed who carries her to the home of the trolls, which is crawling with nasty, fighting, troll children, including her brother who has become one. Bribing the guard by teaching him how to knit, and her brother with her red scarf, she trudges back home with her brother in her arms. She must also carry the red mare, who returned to her former size at daybreak after being wounded by the pursuing trolls. The story is vaguely reminiscent of *The Tombs of Atuan*, in which the brave hero enters the dark tombs and leads an unwilling victim back to the light. Julie Dowling's gorgeous paintings illustrate the cold dimness of a winter lit by the glowing gifts of the red scarf and the magical horse.

Le Guin is a cat lover, and she indulges this long-term affection in several of her books for children. Anne Barrow, the illustrator for *A Visit from Dr. Katz* (1988), used her neighbor's cats as well as her niece's for models. The psychological theme of *Catwings* (1988) is the need of individuals for a peaceful place to thrive. A family of winged kittens is born behind a city dumpster to a single mother in a city where food is scarce, wheels are scary, and the scenery is ugly. Their mother, understanding that their difference makes their lives more dangerous, urges them to escape to a more peaceful environment. After adventures in the woods, where one of them is injured by an owl, they find a home with two kind children who know the importance of letting these kittens live free even while they offer them sustenance and protection. These winged cats are smaller versions of the windsteeds in Le Guin's first published novel, *Rocannon's World,* but their story is far more relevant for young people. Crescent Dragonwings, the renowned reviewer of children's books, compares this book to E. B. White's classic, *Stuart Little,* praising Le Guin's "dialogue, humor, skill as a storyteller and emotional veracity," which combine in "a story that is both contemporary and timeless."[7] Critic Ann Flowers also praises the book, noting the appeal of the "sturdy protectiveness" of kittens Harriet and James and recognizing the book as a "gracious loving tribute to the charm of cats."[8]

The sequel, *Catwings Return* (1989), reiterates the theme of the need for a safe place to grow, especially for people with unique gifts. Two of the cats return to their city, guided by instinct, to visit their mother. There they discover a tiny black kitten, a sister who is also winged but too weak and young to escape from the building where she has landed. After gaining her trust, they lead her back to their mother, now living contentedly as a pet. Their mother assures them of her own happiness and encourages them to return to Overhill Farm, where they can live safely. A good mother lets go.

*Fish Soup* (1992), illustrated by Patrick Wynne, is also about good parenting. The thinking man of Moha who kept his house too neat is contrasted with the sloppy writing woman of Maho. Each has a child. Too much is expected of the man's son, who grows too big, and too little is expected of the woman's daughter, who shrinks. This tale illustrates its moral with wry and gentle wit. Perhaps the winged pet mice who appear in this tale will someday meet the Catwings.

In *Wonderful Alexander and the Catwings* (1994) the young Alexander Furby, proud of his prowess at cat skills, knows he is wonderful until his adventures lead him up a tree too tall for comfort. He is rescued by a shy young kitten with wings but without a mew. The quiet cat leads Alexander back to her family, the Catwings, who explain that Jane, since they rescued her from urban blight, has not made a sound except under extreme duress. Concerned, Alexander uses "tough love" to provoke Jane to talk about her horrid experiences in the city, regaining for himself the title "wonderful."

Most readers, of course, will return to these books more to worry about how these adorable winged kittens will survive the terrors of the cold wet world and to enjoy the relief of their rescue than to figure out deeper meanings. These stories are charmingly comfortable, with just the right rhythms and pacing to keep the cats from becoming too human or too cute. S. D. Schindler's barely tinted ink drawings beautifully reflect Le Guin's psychological realism in these three fantasies, in which the generosity of both animal and human characters illustrates the kind of love that protects and nurtures without restricting freedom, the kind of love also recommended and illustrated in *The Dispossessed, Very Far Away from Anywhere Else,* and the Earthsea series.

In these books for children, as in her recent short stories and poems, Le Guin seems to be moving toward settings and characters whose fantastical elements are grounded in territory familiar to most readers, if not geographically at least psychologically. Even when her stories occur in the future or on places other than Earth, they ring with deep chords of recognition, perhaps because she is moving inward from the realms of myth, politics, and social relationships toward more personal voices.

# 6. Dancing from the Center: *Always Coming Home,* Poetry, *Buffalo Gals and Other Animal Presences, Searoad, A Fisherman of the Inland Sea,* and *Four Ways to Forgiveness*

Ursula K. Le Guin has decried the frequent effort of critics and chroniclers of her work to reduce it to a compendium of ideas or themes. "I do feel that there is a tendency to talk about ideas as if they were all that matters, whereas what matters to me are the characters, the emotions, the relationships, and the music that all those things, plus the sound of the words themselves, make in the reader's mind. My stuff is more like dancing than it is like essays."[1] She is right. Her myths, legends, and imaginative fictions use the symbolic language that reaches beyond what can be articulated easily in language. Especially in her recent work, Le Guin is stepping beyond traditional images and symbols to create dances of sound, image, and the ordinary words of daily lives to connect to readers in other ways. She describes this feminist way of communicating in an essay about the differences between the traditional language of power, which creates distance by separating the speaker and the object being discussed, and the "mother

Le Guin enjoys sharing her views about women's issues, literature, and freedom to choose.
*Courtesy of Marian Wood Kolisch.*

tongue," which connects, unites, and includes: "We went back to
feeling our way into ideas, using the whole intellect not half of it,
talking with one another, which involves listening. We tried to
offer our experience to one another."[2]

*Always Coming Home* is an experiment in using language to share an imaginative experience as wholly as possible by stretching beyond the normal parameters of literature. Le Guin continues to work with other artists to combine media, but she has returned to concentrating on narrative as her main form of communication. However, the voice she uses is more personal and her characters are more ordinary, even in extraordinary settings; her talent is such that these characters and their experiences are no less fascinating than the more traditional protagonists of her previous work. Most likely she would agree with critic Cummins: "Narrative art is to be valued not only for its content, lesson, or entertainment but also for its ability to replicate the communal experience" (185), for that is what her stories do.

## *Always Coming Home*

This book has been called "an archeological dig"[3] into the distant future that "creates an entire culture, not just a cast of characters ... an impressive achievement from an impressive writer,"[4] "a novel with holes in it ... an exchange of gifts, analogous to the act which is the foundation of human community" (Cummins, 195). Indeed it is hard to forget Le Guin's background in anthropology while experiencing this work, which begins with a note to the reader explaining the difficulty of translating a language of the future. Le Guin is inventing a history of the future, an exploration through speculative thinking of people who have not yet lived. Why is this important? Only what can be lived vicariously can become wisely realized; imagining the future makes planning ahead possible. Just as traditional anthropological writers attempt to recreate the past by imaginatively stitching together the threads of story, artifact, and metaphor, Le Guin fabricates a possible future, weaving invented words and sounds, poetry, history, drama, myths, instructions, and a long narrative into a nonlinear yet cohesive experience, reminiscent of some Native American cultures.

In her essay "The Carrier Bag Theory of Fiction," Le Guin contrasts the traditional legend in which a hero overcomes an obstacle, usually by killing it, with the "life story," which is more like a carrier bag that holds human deeds and feelings: "A book holds words. Words hold things. They bear meanings. A novel is a medicine bundle, holding things in a particular powerful relation to one another and to us . . . the Hero . . . needs a stage or a pedestal or a pinnacle."[5] In *Always Coming Home* Le Guin makes such a carrier bag to convey the life story of the Kesh, a people of the future. The book holds the songs, myths, some histories, a long narrative autobiography, several short biographies, poems, informational essays, a glossary of the Kesh language, maps, and elegantly imaginative illustrations by Margaret Chodos. Collaborating with composer Todd Barton, Le Guin recorded the music of the Kesh, which is available on an accompanying audiotape.

Le Guin plays six roles as she tells the story of the Kesh: ethnologist, editor, translator, novelist, the middle-aged housewife Stone Telling, and Pandora.[6] As ethnologist, she gathers and presents information about these people of the valley. This life occurs after the present Industrial Age has depleted much of the fuels and materials currently used. In the middle of this work, the chapter titled "Time and the City" places the Kesh in the future. The section called "Beginnings" (168–170) describes four stages of life on Earth. The first era has no human people but does support "four-legged people"; it ends with meteor showers. The second era ends in floods, similar to those told about in the Biblical story of Noah and in other cultural myths. The third seems to be a description of our current culture, which destroys itself through environmental poisoning. In the fourth, the Kesh and their environment still suffer some of the effects of that destruction. Although the people live in small villages, their accumulated knowledge is stored in a computerized network of information that can be accessed by anybody who requests it; its goal is to "become a total mental model or replica of the Universe" (159) to enable "conscious, self-directed evolution" for those who care to participate, whether the request be for "a recipe for yogurt or for . . . weaponry" (158). Whereas our traditional cultures are organized on linear principles, these people do not pay attention to time nor dates, focusing instead on the inexplicable connection to momentary life and to the eternal, which Le Guin names "the hinge" (160). Our present civilization is described in the story "A Hole in the Air," which paints a picture of "back-ward headed people" ensconced inside, having poisoned their natural environment. The twentieth century has led to people who have spoiled the taste of their food with sprays and buried the streams and soil with concrete and industrial waste. It is a horrifying picture.

The Kesh, the people of the Valley of Na, live communally, sharing the work of raising food and weaving clothes and celebrating the passing of the seasons with dance, song, and chant. Their way of living emphasizes respect for individual development in relationships rather than power and the practice of craftsmanship rather than mass-made technology. It seeks to be in harmony with the Earth and its beings; whenever a killing is necessary, the Kesh recite a ritual apology to keep the thought of interconnection constant in the mind. In their dance, their music, their poetry, their speech, and their manner of living, they try to circle around a center: in Kesh, a vaguely articulated but sharply intuited sense of what is valuable in being. Turning points in the various cycles of living are called hinges and are often marked by dances and other rituals learned and celebrated communally but at the will of each individual. Rather than rules or religion, the Kesh seem to have "a working metaphor. . . . The idea that comes nearest the center of the vision is the House; the sign is the hinged spiral or heyaya-if [the pattern of their lodges]; the word is the word of praise and change, the word at the center, heya!" (52). In one of the romantic tales, "At the Springs of Orlu," people who have left the pattern of the houses are described as lost and thus dangerous; they do things without meaning (113).

Death is a returning to the Earth rather than an end to living. The dead are either burned or buried and their memories are kept green by planting gardens rather than erecting stones (87). Le Guin's poem "The Buzzards" provides a visual metaphor of the Kesh pattern of living: "They turn gyring, / return gyring. / . . . Under the circles / inside the gyre / of nine buzzards, / the center is there" (84).

By contrast, the Condor society is organized in a hierarchy that fosters "aggression, domination, exploitation, and enforced acculturation" (404). Called "the One," it makes war on its neighbors, subverts women's roles in favor of the warrior men, and separates itself from the natural world. The Condor desire for godlike power over others leads to the ultimate destruction of their culture.

Le Guin's mother, Theodora Kroeber, described the last of the Yahi tribe in her wonderfully readable book *Ishi*, an anthropological biography that resurrects a culture from the memories of the main character. Using interviews and documents made when Ishi was brought to the Museum of Anthropology and Ethnology at the University of California, where her husband, Alfred Kroeber, was curator, she wrote a book that carefully maintains Ishi's point of view as he moves from his own childhood world into a more technologically advanced culture. As translator, Le Guin uses a similar narrative and viewpoint in a major portion of *Always Coming Home* to help the reader compare two cultures from within the mind of a single character.

As in the Earthsea series, names reflect various stages of living: the narrator is now named Stone Telling because she is recording her own part of the whole story and she is "sitting like a stone" (7) in her home in the Valley. Just as "the present stone contains the absent mountain" (98), a single story can bring to mind intimations of many lives. Originally named by her mother North Owl, after the bird that frequented her childhood home, the young girl remembers how separate she felt because her father was a stranger to the Valley, a Condor who has been away for nine years. The other children tease her because she has no father in the home and she is slow at learning.

The narrative opens with the first of the young girl's three journeys, each encompassing a different type of knowledge and representing a different stage of self-development. Eight-year-old North Owl accompanies her mother and grandmother out of their small village, Sinshan, to the hot springs in Kastoha-na. On this trip, she first sees the larger towns and cities where cousins and other relatives live and becomes aware of her family's history, especially the fact that her father is a Condor and comes from outside the established houses, or lodges, of the Kesh. This "journey of the still air" (10) is North Owl's first venture outward whereby she compares her new experiences and then returns home a fuller person. Soon after, she undertakes a four-day journey alone to Sinshan Mountain, where she seeks wisdom from the four-footed people she meets. The coyote is most welcoming to her and, when she goes home, she knows she has achieved some wisdom from the trip. When her Condor father returns to the Valley with his army, she recognizes his weaknesses even as she is attracted to his influence. However, this sense of herself is confused by the turbulence of adolescence. After her mother rejects her father, Owl consents to accompany him to his land away from the Valley, taking the name of Terter Ayatu, which denotes her new status as the daughter of a Condor leader.

The Condor's goal is to reflect the One, a god who made the world and dominates it. To reflect Him like a mirror, the Condor men strive to be pure, that is, to live apart from all other worldly existence (214). For the Kesh, this separation of the physical and mental, animate from inanimate, workers and thinkers, is wrong: "The hand that shapes the mind into clay or written word slows the thought to the gait of things and lets it be subject to accident and time. Purity is the edge of evil, they say" (185). As a Condor's daughter, Ayatu becomes enslaved by the rigid social restrictions that keep her inside, ignorant, and isolated. She misses the dances and the work of the Valley. More to escape boredom, she marries and has a daughter she names Ekwerkwe, a word for quail. Then, when 10 non-Condors are executed to avenge the deaths of 10 Condors, Ayatu decides to escape with her daughter. Finally understanding Owl's need to return to the Valley, her father arranges for her to get away, and she takes on the name "Woman Coming Home" for the middle of her life. Back in the Valley, she spends the rest of her life making a home for her child and mother, learning the crafts that earn her a comfortable living, entoning the songs, dancing the Dances, eventually marrying again, and enjoying the wealth that allows her to be generous. Now that she is writing this history, she has become Stone Telling.

Le Guin imitates traditional archeology in several technical-sounding reports that describe the physical aspects of the Kesh. "The Serpentine Codex" explains the Valley people's societal structure, which is reflected in their buildings, their annual celebrations, and in their image of the universe. Their geography is delineated in a chapter titled "Where It Is" and by several maps in "The Back of the Book," an appendix that also includes notes about medical practices, clothing, food, dances, playing, love, and language. "Dancing the Moon" (257) describes an annual celebration of sexual pleasures without personal commitment for adults who wish to participate. "How to Die in the Valley" emphasizes the close connection the Kesh have to Earth and its eternal rhythms. "Time and the City" explains the Kesh relationship to both historical and universal time in a short series of texts. "Four Histories" and "Eight Life Stories" provide a wide range of examples of how the Kesh write about themselves and the events that occur. Much of these writings sounds more like fantasy to the contemporary reader than traditional history or biography, but modern archeologists realize that the definition of "reality" differs among cultures. Perhaps what can be imagined is as true as memories of events experienced physically.

*Always Coming Home* also includes numerous artistic works attributed to the Kesh. Literary works are considered gifts from their creator and are received with gratitude. Characters include both animals and humans (both called "people" in the Kesh language, and both considered equally valid as storytellers). Some of the stories for adults contain sexual humor as well as insults and jokes; others contain mystical visions and images. One of the "flytings," or insults, illustrates this kind of earthy humor in Kesh literature: "Great minds prefer strong flavors. / In Chumo they like strong beer, / so they use cat turds" (76). Both the "Four Romantic Tales" and the passage from the novel, "The Dangerous People," center around relationships between lovers. The plots of the "Dramatic Works" are loosely organized to allow the actors to add and interpret according to their intended effect.

Four sections of poetry appear in the book, some folk songs and others lyric and narrative. The lines tend to be short with irregular rhythms and little rhyme but have many repeated words and chantlike stanzas. Le Guin explains that some of the words that seem meaningless are used to remind the singers of ideas that are larger than words. "Heya" encompasses all that is "visible and invisible, on this side and on the other side of death" (98). In addition, the book's accompanying audiotape contains poems performed in the Kesh language with music composed by Todd Barton. Some of these poems are also similar to chants, although the accompanying music is sweetly lyrical and softly rhythmic.

Interspersed among all these texts are short messages from the author's persona, Pandora, who frets about what she is trying to do in this book but is driven by the vision of the dying Earth. Finally she celebrates with the other "owners" of this composition, including the faithful dog, the Geomancer.

In the guise of Pandora, the woman of Greek mythology who released anxieties into the world—probably by raising troubling questions—Le Guin explains that rather than looking over a map of the Valley laid out, she wants to feel and hold and hear the life with a sense that is "not intellectual, but mental. Not spiritual, but heavy. . . . Let the heart compare the pattern" (56). Is *Always Going Home* a novel, science fiction, or fantasy, or does it matter? In "A Brief Note and Chart Concerning Narrative Modes," Le Guin breaks down the differences among realistic literary genres into "What Happened" and "Like What Happened"; all else are "Lies and Jokes" (536). Perhaps this is a more useful delineation of genre than the traditional classifications, for like much of her other work, *Always Coming Home* contains more than ideas. This work is to be experienced, weighed, felt, tasted, fingered, put back, and taken out again rather than read straight through like most other books. Pandora presents this experience to raise questions, yes, but she also hints at answers that give us hope: We still have time to learn about the poisons in our environment, to reach out for global peace and the end of war, to reduce overpopulation, and to use technology wisely. Le Guin makes us feel the urgency of these problems, but also offers a vicarious solution. With Pandora, we learn the Valley mentally, not intellectually; it weighs upon our consciousness.

Since composing this long work, Le Guin has published an addition to the Earthsea series, *Tehanu,* discussed in chapter 3, several books for children, and several collections of short stories and poetry. These volumes all embody her continuing experimentation with language as a way to bypass the conscious and speak to a consciousness more inclusive than mere intellect; they celebrate her increasing awareness of feminist theory and her concern for pollution and waste of our natural resources.

## Poetry

Le Guin's venture to communicate beyond the mere intellect, to learn to dance with language, began early, when she started writing poetry at about the age of five: "A poem tends to begin with a sort of beat in the mind to which words fit themselves."[7] In her essay "Reciprocity of Prose and Poetry," Le Guin acknowledges the difficulty in differentiating between the two. The aesthete's idea that "poetry is the beautiful dumb blond, all sound, and prose is the smart brunette with glasses, all sense"[8] is inadequate, for both forms of writing contain both sound and sense. Yet whereas prose can be translated, poetry becomes something else when its words are changed. At any rate, poetry expresses moods, celebrates and grieves, puts readers in tune with the connections between sound, shape, and sense in ways that prose cannot do. In the same essay, Le Guin notes that because she was first recognized as a prose writer, her poetry is often dismissed as a secondary effort.

*Wild Angels,* published in 1975, is the first collection of her poetry and is dedicated to the memory of her father, Alfred Kroeber, who died in 1960. Most of the 30 poems center around the themes of nature, death, family, and her personal experiences as a writer. These first experiments in catching the language of poetry use a "hard, compact, tense . . . sparse surface . . . deepened by mythic roots rather than elaborated by figures of speech" (Spivack, 137). These poems expose less of her enthusiasm than her later work. In 1979, Le Guin collaborated with her mother, Theodora Kroeber Quinn, on a small collection of poetry titled

*Tillai and Tylissos,* which explores the metaphor of dance. *Hard Words and Other Poems* (1981) includes some of these poems, along with more poetry about the difficult work of finding the right word, words that speak with the power of their mythic connotations. Another small volume, *In the Red Zone* (1983), is illustrated by Henk Pander. Another poetic collaboration is *Blue Moon over Thurman Street* (1993), a celebration of the many people, sights, and mental reactions available in Le Guin's own neighborhood, combining her words with the photographs of Roger Dorband.

*Wild Oats and Fireweed* (1988) reflects Le Guin's identification with the vegetable world, her insistence that humans resist thinking of the "natural" environment as other or separate from ourselves.[9] Her use of puns ("I will be welling," 86), near rhymes and alliteration (the "bony, piny sandy silence" of Georgia, 86), and repetition ("I have borne, I have borne, I have borne," 68) synchronize the rhythms of human life with the sounds and images of the Earth. *Going out with Peacocks and Other Poems* (1994) illustrates Le Guin's most recent directions. More political than the contents of her previous volumes, some of the poetry addresses AIDS, domestic violence, the First Amendment, and the threat of the atom bomb. Other poems express the complex patterns of domesticity and family relationships. The last section, "Dancing on the Sun," encourages readers to "leap higher and higher into the dark / until you somersault to sleep,"[10] that is, toward the mysterious and the spiritual. Reviewer Alan Frank called it "an album of gracious verse," and indeed Le Guin's voice has become more confident and daring, honest, and direct, using "a bright flood"[11] of imagery, ideas, and voice. Similar voices emerge in her recent collections of short works.

## Buffalo Gals and Other Animal Presences

The title piece of this collection of stories and poetry, "Buffalo Gals," was reprinted with illustrations by Susan Boulet that emphasize the "fit and fumble of animal/human interaction,"[12] the general topic uniting these short pieces. Boulet draws the coyote of the story with a half human body, clarifying the possible parallel between a young girl's family and the animal community that welcomes her when she is stranded in the desert after a plane crash. In "Mazes," a laboratory alien (animal?) views the experimenter with what we usually call a "human," or even "humanitarian," viewpoint. The story "May's Lion" is told in two ways, describing alternate ways of handling potentially destructive meetings between human and animal beasts. This volume also includes reprints of "Vaster Than Empires and More Slow" from *The Wind's Twelve Quarters* and "Schrödinger's Cat" from *The Compass Rose*. Le Guin introduces each of the 11 sections as if she were going to read them aloud, allowing commentary on pacing, emphasis, and other aspects of story usually bypassed in literary discussions. Reviews were generally positive, noting Le Guin's tremendous talent with language but sometimes complaining about her enthusiasm for feminist and environmental issues: her poetry celebrates women, children, cats, and the natural world in "hosannas against the threat of male power and destructiveness ... which both exasperate and exhilarate her audience";[13] "more treat than trick ... [she expresses herself] in writing too solemn for its theme" (O'Rourke, 38). These stories offer thought-provoking insights and pose important questions on two topics particularly vital for young people today—the endangered environment and gender equity. The next collection centers more on another stage of life.

## *Searoad: Chronicles of Klatsand*

"Foam Women, Rain Women," the short piece that introduces this collection, sets the place and the mood. The place is the Northwest, the cold, windy, wet edge of civilization, where women either find themselves dispersed by the relentless motion of living or rise tall and disperse themselves at will. "I guess we think when a woman's free, she's wrong,"[14] says Jane, who represents the middle generation of the Hernes, the family of women anchoring this collection. But she's just admitted that her daughter and her mother have made good choices. Foam women can rise and become rain women, bringing delight, allowing creation, like the love goddess Venus born from the ocean as portrayed so beautifully by Botticelli's "Birth of Venus."

But the stories are not as ethereal as this framing image. Personal and intimate, particular in detail, these portraits are told from within the minds of several inhabitants of Klatsand, the seaside village along the edge of the western shore. They contain the pettiness and the wonder, the love and the bitterness, the courage and the fear of most minds who live as individuals within a community. The inhabitants of Klatsand work in hotels, stay in motels, have been to war, nurse the sick, fool with crafts, talk about each other, are kind, are cruel, are the range of humans we expect to live in a small seaside village, yet never know as well as these stories tell. The final, long piece, "Hernes," consists of diary entries from four generations of the Herne women, ranging from Fanny, one of the first settlers of Klatsand in 1898, to Virginia, who in 1983 wins the Pulitzer Prize for her feminist poetry. These entries, though not in chronological order nor a comprehensive history, bring together people from the other stories in the same way a mind makes a community of individuals met in a lifetime, though dispersed in time. Thus, although the stories can be read separately (and except for "Foam Women" and "Hernes" were individually published elsewhere), they also work in harmony, similar to several of Le Guin's other recent collections, united more by place than by time and more by similar patterns and rhythms than by conceptual themes.

Although many critics praised this collection for the memorable, complex characters painted so intricately and convincingly, several focused their comments on the book's feminist themes. Le Guin makes several references to the myth of Persephone. This young goddess is raped and kidnapped by Hades, and her mother's grief and anger results in winter for half the year, the time Persephone stays in Hades's realm. Men in this novel are often violent, or weak in other ways. These are the kinds of stories Le Guin has urged women to tell, so their lives, unheralded in other public ways, will not disappear from memory.

Isobel Armstrong notes that *Searoad* has the "'radial' structure, anti-realist and atemporal,"[15] more common in folk epic than in written literature, as the characters, setting, and plot can be either fully delineated or completely absent. The characters are ordinary people not traditionally individuated—waitresses, cleaning maids, housewives, craftsmen, people usually silent in public. Le Guin's involvement with feminist issues is well-known, but her stories are more than illustrations of her ideas. Like the children of the mothers she depicts and like all stories, these tales are creations that take on a life of their own in the minds of each reader.

## A Fisherman of the Inland Sea

In her introduction to *A Fisherman of the Inland Sea* (1994), Le Guin complains that many critics and readers tend to read science fiction for the message or the main idea. "They are not fortune cookies. They are stories,"[16] she writes, reiterating that the experience of reading good literature involves more than abstracting the theme or the main idea; it is also appreciating the beauty of the work, the beauty of its form or its morality or even its humor. All fictions widen our experience, transposing us out of our present time, place, or mind set into new areas of imagined thought. Science fiction merely uses technology to extend the parameters of our imaginations. In this collection, Le Guin questions the nature of narrative and how it changes when we shift viewpoints or allow ourselves to share viewpoints.

The first story, "The First Contact with the Gorgonids," depicts the stereotypical "ugly American tourist" who believes a story that his wife intuits may not be the truth as he sees it. Told in talk-show language, the story is satisfying and funny, a traditional tale of the victorious victim. "Newton's Sleep" is a poignant story of Ike, a father who painfully comes to realize the inadequacy of neat, pure technology and the "superclean military worldlet" (10) it can produce for humans who thrive on difference and dirt. Le Guin explains that the title is from poet William

Blake's wish that we avoid "single vision and Newton's sleep" (10). The third short story, like the first, is a light-hearted inversion of our expectations. "The Rock That Changed Things" is a meditative parable about freedom and viewpoint in which a dominant people establishes a formal pattern, a way of viewing the world that lacks the richer, more colorful visions of their servants, whom they deem intellectually inferior. This story again challenges the idea that simplicity and order is adequate for a full human life. "The Kerastion" is a story Le Guin expanded from a writers' workshop invention by Roussel Sargent, "a musical instrument that cannot be heard" (10) but is played at funerals for the dead to hear and understand. In this story, Le Guin expands on a concept from *Always Coming Home*—that the process of creating and appreciating is more important than the artifact, which will, in time, deteriorate and return to its source, the Earth.

The last three stories center around Le Guin's "churten" theory, which allows space travel without a lapse in time. The theory is a metaphor for the power of the imagination to weave a story from all the sensations that constantly bombard us. In "The Shobies' Story," the 10 travelers escape from chaos by telling their parts of the story and are able to return to the familiar. They had discovered that when participants make an effort to agree on their perceptions of what is happening, or of their stories, they can rescue coherence from chaos. In "Dancing to Ganam," one of four space travelers, Dalzul, tells himself a story that differs from what the other three see; Dalzul's delusion, and the fact that he will not hear the stories of the others, leads to a shocking conclusion. In "Another Story," Le Guin explores the possibility of living two stories at once, through the technology of time travel.

*A Fisherman of the Inland Sea* is an intellectually challenging exploration of the implications of the constructivist theory of language and the power of stories in our lives. The title may refer to her writing process, which she describes as translating from "the source, the deep sea where ideas swim, and one catches them in nets of words and swings them shining into the boat" ("Reciprocity of Prose and Poetry," 112). Or it may refer to the inland sea described in *Always Coming Home* formed by earthquakes on the western coast of North America. The creator of stories fishes into the mind to try to ascertain how we keep our lives together. But the mind is broader than the intellect, which, like the obls in "The Rock That Changed Things," seeks order first. The mind is more inclusive of the complexities of emotion, image, color, and individual memory. These stories themselves capture those complexities, offering experiences full of color, pattern, emotional surges, and, yes, beauty. In this collection, Le Guin illustrates her ability to weave the thread of a theory or an idea into a story of memorable characters and surprises.

## Four Ways to Forgiveness

In a review of *Searoad,* reviewer Monroe Engel worried that Le Guin would feel that she had a "feminist responsibility to write realist fiction" and would abandon science fiction.[17] Instead, in *Four Ways to Forgiveness* (1995), Le Guin uses science fiction to explore issues that arise from feminist thinking, in this case the impact of the master-slave relationship on all members of a strictly hierarchical society. As the French philosopher Theodoré Rousseau explained in *The Social Contract,* masters are as trapped by the master-slave relationship as their slaves. The four novellas take place on two neighboring planets, described in the book's endnotes in historical detail similar to the anthropological data in *Always Coming Home.* On the planet Werel, black-skinned people from the southern part of the continent Voe Deo conquered and enslaved the white-skinned inhabitants of the north, establishing a society based on slavery that has existed for about 3,000 years. When Werel colonized the uninhabited planet Yeowe, it exported its system of slavery to that planet. About 60 years before the story's time, an uprising of slave women angered by the repeated rape of girl-children began the War of Liberation, which ended with the defeat and expulsion of the Werelians from Yeowe. Unfortunately, the first attempts at self-rule failed, and several years afterward, despite the help of the

Ekumen, the government is still shaky. As reviewer Jonas points out, this political saga is told in anything but political terms. Le Guin uses the "mother language" she described in *Dancing at the Edge of the World* to tell this story, "honing in on the individuals and the roles they play, by choice or not, in the great events of history."[18] Each of the four sections tells part of the historical event, a personal slice of the truth that is richer than a mere part of the whole but is also always less than the whole.

The first section describes the gradual growth of a relationship between a former school administrator, Yoss, and the deposed Chief Abberkam, accused of betraying the Liberation cause in its first years of trying to establish a stable government. Yoss has retired to the marshes, determined to spend the rest of her life in silence, studying the scriptures of the Arkamye and denying herself all but the simplest of earthly pleasures. However, her mind is too interested in the people around her and her body too drawn to the comforts of wine, warmth, and sweets for her to be a successful martyr. Instead, she spends her energy in acts of comfort and kindness, including nursing Abberkam out of his illness and his guilt. When her house burns down, the aging chief rescues her cat and invites her to stay with him. Perhaps they have betrayed their noble intentions to serve an ideal, but in their humble acts of generosity toward each other, they find the peace of mutual acceptance and forgiveness.

The second story, "Forgiveness Day," traces the development of a deep understanding between a member of the Owner class and a worldly young woman who scorns the whole class system, especially slavery. Solly, a "space brat" (35) and the first envoy of the Ekumen to the Werel planet Gatay, feels lonely, distanced by the habitual suspicions of the servants who surround her and by the formality of her official hosts, all men at a loss about how to treat a woman who thinks and acts as if she were equal. Much to the horror of her hosts, especially the stiffly disapproving soldier hired to guard her, she has an affair with Batikam, a transvestite actor of the slave caste. However, soon she finds that he too is more obedient than sincere, for without freedom, he cannot afford to be honest. Yet Batikam appreciates her effort to transgress the rigid boundaries of class and later rescues her from imprisonment.

At the Festival of Forgiveness, Solly is kidnapped along with her guard. During their internment, they first learn to honor each other and then to love. The highly disciplined soldier Teyeo understands how trapped he and his fellow Owners are by the necessity of masters to keep control: "We learn to ... close ranks ... ; it wastes energy, the spirit" (79). In turn, Solly, the envoy with the idealistically democratic ideals, formerly so confident of the Ekumen's moral superiority, recognizes the presumptuousness of their mission: "Blundering into your soul ... [w]e *are* invaders, no matter how pacifist and priggish we are" (89). "Forgiveness Day" traces first the increasing friction of these representatives of such separate cultures until an explosion at the festival and then describes the melting warmth afterward as they learn to forgive each other's differences. Winner of the *Asimov's* Readers' Award for 1995 and the Sturgeon Award for Best Short Fiction, it is a heartwarming love story and a fable about erasing intolerable differences by listening empathetically.

"A Man of the People" depicts the way a single person can change a culture, not by rebelling violently, but by asking questions that "change a soul" (143). Havzhiva is a member of a small tribe in the village of Stse, where women share power with men and all are happy and at peace with their choices. Content at first in his partnership with Iyan Iyan, he becomes fascinated with a different way of knowing than he has been taught. He wants to study history, a kind of knowledge that describes a reality in a language other than what he has heard in the village, so he goes to the School at Kathhad. From there, he is sent as an envoy to the planet Yeowe, which is still recovering from its recent War of Liberation. He asks unsettling questions about the ways these newly liberated slaves still subjugate their women, even retaining a ritualized rape of young girls, the very act that purportedly instigated the first rebellion of the female slaves against their masters. As a stranger to this culture, Havzhiva realizes he can see the larger historical patterns but cannot perceive the particular designs of the whole picture. Only those who live within a culture can fully comprehend the local rules; only they can sense the most beneficial pace for change. Still, he has been useful to the women of Yeowe, for his presence as an alien has raised questions about the larger implications of their cultural practices. Recognizing the limitations of what he can see, both as a stranger to another culture and as a member of his own, Havzhiva forgives himself for not knowing everything. His acceptance of life's imperfections has helped him learn to walk with his own people, as well as with strangers in other worlds.

"A Woman's Liberation" explores "the nature of servitude and the nature of freedom" (145). Rakam, though as dark-skinned as the Owners, begins her life as the pampered pet of the mistress of the Shomeke plantation, her body and mind wholly obedient to the whims of the lady she knows only to adore. Born into slavery, Rakam has never learned anything but reverence for and obedience to the Owners. Not until she and the other Assets are granted their freedom papers by Lord Erod, who inherits Shomeke, does Rakam begin to realize how difficult freedom is to maintain. Recaptured almost immediately, she serves at another plantation before she escapes to the city, where she learns to read and to study history. Her popularity as a public speaker for women's equal rights makes the city dangerous for her. A stranger from Ekumen helps her escape the threat of political imprisonment to Yeowe, where, after a stint working in the rice paddies, she travels to a city where she again speaks out in support of women's equality. Finally she meets a man she can love of her own free will, forgiving all who have abused her by forcing acts of lust upon her body with no attention to her will.

Against the huge span of history, of horrible cruelty and great battles, love between two people seems a small thing. "But a key is a little thing, next to the door it opens. . . . It is in our bodies that we accept or begin our freedom" (208). The four ways to forgiveness all lead to "the one noble thing," an honest love between two individuals, the key to peace and freedom that opens the door from ignorance and self-absorption. Most critics have reviewed this book favorably, recognizing the rich resonance of Le Guin's prose and the relevance of her ideas to present political situations.

Le Guin's thinking and writing traces a circular recursive road as, in her latest works, she returns to the metaphor of science fiction and fantastic language. The alien-sounding names that once invited readers to explore foreign shores now draw them deeper into the landscape of the mind to define how individual selves are formed and how they might be most honestly and fully expressed. A critic at *Publishers Weekly* sums up Le Guin's intellectual impact in a review of *A Fisherman of the Inland Sea,* which launched a new imprint from the publisher HarperCollins. HarperPrism offers a line of books acknowledging the permanent value of science fiction/fantasy with hardback versions of the best of this often marginalized genre. "Le Guin ponders the nature of art and how life should be lived," the art of living well, in harmony with the Earth and with others. The recurring themes of her work include the "ability of power to corrupt the once well-intended" and, as if in answer, a "celebration of cultural diversity, of unlikely heroes and heroines, and, finally and most usefully, love's power to guide."[19] However, only the reader who spends the time and attention to experience Le Guin's work—the myths, the science fiction stories, the political novels, the poetry, the dramatic works, the essays, the whole shebang or just a piece—will appreciate the full impact of the dance she choreographs and performs, weaving together the power of the unconscious symbolic myth with the beauty of intellectual surprise, the language of the mother as well as that of the father.

# Notes and References

## 1. *Ursula K. Le Guin: Dancing Weaver*

1. Ursula K. Le Guin, "Theodora." Reprinted in *Dancing at the Edge of the World* (New York: Grove, 1989), 138; hereafter cited in the text.

2. Paul Mandelbaum, "Ursula K. Le Guin," *First Words* (Chapel Hill, NC: Algonquin Books, 1993), 316.

3. Anne Fadiman, "Ursula K. Le Guin: Voyager to the Inner Land," *Life* 9, no. 4 (April 1986): 24; hereafter cited in the text.

4. Joe De Bolt, *Ursula K. Le Guin: Voyager to Inner Lands and to Outer Space* (Port Washington, NY: Kennikat Press, 1979), 15.

5. Anne Commire, ed., *Something About the Author* (Detroit: Gale Research, 1987), 52, 102.

6. Ursula K. Le Guin, "Citizen of Mondath," 1973. Reprinted in *The Language of the Night* (New York: Perigee, 1979), 26.

7. Keddy Outlaw, "Home Again, Home Again," *Wilson Library Bulletin* (December 1994): 120.

8. Maureen Dezell, "Ursula K. Le Guin: Still Toying with Fantasy, Reality," *Boston Globe* (3 August 1994): 70.

9. William Walsh, "I Am a Woman Writer; I Am a Western Writer: An Interview with Ursula K. Le Guin," *Kenyon Review* (Summer 1995): 194.

10. Miriam Berkley, "Ursula K. Le Guin," *Publishers Weekly* (23 May 1986): 72.

11. Ursula K. Le Guin, "Dreams Must Explain Themselves," *The Language of the Night* (New York: Perigee, 1979), 55.

12. Barbara Bucknall, *Ursula K. Le Guin* (New York: Frederick Ungar, 1981), 8.

13. Jonathan White, "Coming Back from the Silence," *Whole Earth Review* (Spring 1985): 82.

14. Paul Bauman, "So Many Books, So Little Time," *Commonweal* (11 August 1989): 441.

15. Ursula K. Le Guin, "Room 9. Car 1430," reprinted in *Dancing at the Edge of the World* (New York: Grove, 1989), 135–137.

**2. *Learning the Hainish Dance:***
**Rocannon's World, Planet of Exile, *and* City of Illusions**

1. Ursula K. Le Guin, "Escape Routes," *The Language of the Night* (New York: Perigee, 1979), 206.

2. Ursula K. Le Guin, "A Citizen of Mondath," *The Language of the Night* (New York: Perigee, 1979), 28.

3. Elizabeth Cummins, *Understanding Ursula K. Le Guin* (Columbia, SC: University of South Carolina, 1990), 68.

4. Ian Watson, "Le Guin's *Lathe of Heaven* and the Role of Dick: The False Reality as Mediator," *Science-Fiction Studies* 2 (March 1975): 68.

5. James Bittner, *Approaches to the Fiction of Ursula K. Le Guin* (Ann Arbor, MI: UMI Research Press, 1984; Essex: Bowker, 1984), 91.

6. Ursula K. Le Guin, *The Dispossessed: An Ambiguous Utopia* (New York: Harper & Row, 1974), 381; hereafter cited in the text.

7. Ursula K. Le Guin, "Vaster Than Empires and More Slow," *The Wind's Twelve Quarters* (New York: Bantam, 1976), 167.

8. Ursula K. Le Guin, *Rocannon's World* (New York: Ace, 1966), 5.

9. Ursula K. Le Guin, *City of Illusions* (New York: Ace, 1967), 1; hereafter cited in the text.

10. Ursula K. Le Guin, "A Citizen of Mondath," *The Language of the Night* (New York: Perigee, 1979), 28.

11. Ursula K. Le Guin, "Introduction to *Rocannon's World*," reprinted in *The Language of the Night* (New York: Perigee, 1979), 135.

**3. *The Earthsea Cycle, a New Dance for Legendary Tunes:***
**A Wizard of Earthsea, The Tombs of Atuan, The Farthest Shore, *and* Tehanu**

1. *Contemporary Literary Criticism* (Detroit: Gale Research, 1992), 71, 177.

2. Ursula K. Le Guin, "Dreams Must Explain Themselves," *The Language of the Night* (New York: Perigee, 1979), 51; hereafter cited in the text.

3. Ursula K. Le Guin, *A Wizard of Earthsea* (New York: Ace, 1970), 52; hereafter cited in the text.

4. Ursula K. Le Guin, "The Child and the Shadow," *The Language of the Night* (New York: Perigee, 1979), 65.

5. Craig and Diana Barrow, "Le Guin's Earthsea: Voyages in Consciousness," *Extrapolation* (Spring 1991): 22–23.

6. Margaret Esmonde, "The Master Pattern: The Psychological Journey in the Earthsea Trilogy," in Joseph Olander and Martin Greenberg, eds., *Ursula K. Le Guin* (New York: Taplinger, 1979), 21–23.

7. Bruno Bettelheim, *The Uses of Enchantment: The Meaning and Importance of Fairy Tales* (New York: Random House, 1989), 212.

8. Ursula K. Le Guin, *The Tombs of Atuan* (New York: Ace, 1971), 10; hereafter cited in the text.

9. Holly Littlefield, "Unlearning Patriarchy: Ursula K. Le Guin's Feminist Consciousness in *The Tombs of Atuan* and *Tehanu*," *Extrapolation* (Fall 1995): 248.

10. Ursula K. Le Guin, *The Farthest Shore* (New York: Atheneum, 1972), 4; hereafter cited in the text.

11. "A Hole in the World," *Times Literary Supplement* (6 April 1973): 3709.

12. Shippey, T. A., "The Magic Art and the Evolution of Works: Ursula K. Le Guin's Earthsea Trilogy," *Mosaic* 10 (Winter 1977): 158.

13. Ursula K. Le Guin, *Tehanu: The Last Book of Earthsea* (New York: Atheneum, 1990), 37.

14. Ursula K. Le Guin, "Children, Women, Men and Dragons," in *Earthsea Revisioned* (Cambridge: Green Bay, 1993), 21.

15. Dennis O'Brien, *Commonweal* (9 December 1977): 25.

16. John Clute, "Deconstructing Paradise," *Times Literary Supplement* (28 December 1990): 1409.

17. Michael Dirda, "Tehanu," *Book World* (25 February 1990): 9.

18. Robin McKinley, "The Woman Wizard's Triumph," *New York Times Book Review* (12 May 1990): 38.

19. Meredith Tax, "Tehanu," *Village Voice* (25 February 1990): 75.

20. Ursula K. Le Guin, "The Child and the Shadow," *The Language of the Night* (New York: Perigee, 1979), 62.

## 4. Connecting the Hainish Dance and Collective Power: The Left Hand of Darkness, The Lathe of Heaven, The Word for World Is Forest, *and* The Dispossessed

1. Ursula K. Le Guin, *The Wind's Twelve Quarters: Short Stories* (New York: Harper & Row, 1975), 106.

2. Ursula K. Le Guin, *The Left Hand of Darkness* (New York: Ace, 1969), 12; hereafter cited in the text.

3. Ursula K. Le Guin, "Is Gender Necessary? Redux," *Dancing at the Edge of the World: Thoughts on Words, Women, Places* (New York: Grove, 1989), 8.

4. Douglas Barbour, "The Lathe of Heaven: Taoist Dream," *Algol* 21 (November 1973): 22–24.

5. Ursula K. Le Guin, *The Lathe of Heaven* (New York: Scribner's Sons, 1971), 30.

6. Ursula K. Le Guin, *The Word for World Is Forest* (New York: Putnam, 1976), 7; hereafter cited in the text.

7. Ursula K. Le Guin, *The Wind's Twelve Quarters* (New York: Harper & Row, 1975), 260.

8. Ursula K. Le Guin, *The Dispossessed: An Ambiguous Utopia* (New York: Harper & Row, 1974), 27; hereafter cited in the text.

9. Ursula K. Le Guin, "The Ones Who Walk Away from Omelas," *The Wind's Twelve Quarters* (New York: Harper & Row, 1975), 18.

10. Examples include "Authors' Choices," *New York Times Magazine* (14 November 1993): 10, and "The Nature of Things," *New York Times Book Review* (11 July 1993): 14.

### 5. *Orsinia and Other Far Away Places:*
### The Wind's Twelve Quarters, Orsinian Tales, The Eye of the Heron, Malafrena, Very Far Away from Anywhere Else, The Beginning Place, The Rose Compass, *and Stories for Children*

1. Virginia Kidd, ed., *Millennial Women* (New York: Dell, 1978). Virginia Kidd has worked with Le Guin as her agent for many years and has helped her edit several collections.

2. Ursula K. Le Guin, *Very Far Away from Anywhere Else* (New York: Atheneum, 1976), 5.

3. Ursula K. Le Guin, *The Beginning Place* (New York: Harper & Row, 1980), 119.

4. Andrew Gordon, "Ursula K. Le Guin," *Dictionary of Literary Biography* (Detroit: Gale Research, 1986), 52, 240.

5. E. F. Bleiler, "Ursula K. Le Guin," *Supernatural Fiction Writers* (New York: Scribners, 1985), 1064.

6. Ursula K. Le Guin, "Why Are Americans Afraid of Dragons?" *The Language of the Night* (New York: Perigee, 1979), 44.

7. Crescent Dragonwings, "Upper Mobility in the Kitty Ghetto," *New York Times Book Review* (13 November 1988): 40.

8. Ann Flowers, "Catwings," *The Horn Book* (March 1989): 206.

9. Charlotte Spivack, *Ursula K. Le Guin* (Boston: Twayne Publishers, 1984), 83.

### 6. *Dancing from the Center:*
### Always Coming Home, Poetry, Buffalo Gals and Other Animal Presences, Searoad, A Fisherman of the Inland Sea, *and* Four Ways to Forgiveness

1. Letter from Ursula K. Le Guin, November 1995.

2. Ursula K. Le Guin, "Bryn Mawr Commencement Address," *Dancing at the Edge of the World* (New York: Grove, 1989), 150.

3. Brian D. Johnson, "Always Coming Home," *Maclean's Magazine* (4 November 1985): 72.

4. H. J. Kirchhoff, *Toronto Globe & Mail* (7 December 1985): 195.

5. Ursula K. Le Guin, "The Carrier Bag Theory of Fiction," *Dancing at the Edge of the World* (New York: Grove, 1989), 169.

6. Ursula K. Le Guin, *Always Coming Home* (New York: Harper & Row, 1985), 156–182; hereafter cited in the text.

7. Ursula K. Le Guin, "Interview with Jean W. Ross," *Contemporary Authors* 32(1991): 252.

8. Ursula K. Le Guin, "Reciprocity of Prose and Poetry," *Dancing at the Edge of the World* (New York: Grove, 1989), 109.

9. Ursula K. Le Guin, *Wild Oats and Fireweed: New Poems* (New York: Harper & Row, 1988), 67; hereafter cited in the text.

10. Ursula K. Le Guin, *Going out with Peacocks and Other Poems* (New York: HarperCollins, 1994), 82.

11. Frank Allen, *Library Journal* (1 June 1994): 110.

12. Rebecca O'Rourke, *New Statesman & Society* (16 March 1990): 38.

13. *Publishers Weekly* (24 July 1987): 176.

14. Ursula K. Le Guin, *Searoad: Chronicles of Klatsand* (New York: HarperCollins, 1991), 196.

15. Isobel Armstrong, "Searoad," *Times Literary Supplement* (13 March 1992): 23.

16. Ursula K. Le Guin, *A Fisherman of the Inland Sea* (New York: HarperPrism, 1994), 6.

17. Monroe Engel, "Searoad," *New York Times Book Review* (12 January 1992): 10.

18. Gerald Jonas, "Science Fiction," *New York Times Book Review* (15 October 1995): 33.

19. "Review of *A Fisherman of the Inland Sea*," *Publishers Weekly* (28 November 1994): 47.

# Selected Bibliography

## Primary Works

### Novels

*Always Coming Home.* (Includes tape cassette of "Music and Poetry of the Kesh," with music by Todd Barton; illustrations by Margaret Chodos; diagrams by George Hersh.) New York: Harper & Row, 1985; London: Gollancz, 1986. Reprint without cassette. New York: Bantam, 1987.

*The Beginning Place.* New York: Harper & Row, 1980. Published as *Threshold.* London: Gollancz, 1980; New York: Bantam, 1981.

*City of Illusions.* New York: Ace Books, 1967; London: Gollancz, 1971; New York: Harper & Row, 1978.

*The Dispossessed: An Ambiguous Utopia.* New York: Harper & Row, 1974; London: Gollancz, 1974; New York: Avon, 1975.

*The Eye of the Heron.* New York: Delacorte, 1978; London: Panther-Granada, 1980; New York: Bantam, 1983.

*The Farthest Shore.* New York: Atheneum, 1972; London: Gollancz, 1973; New York: Bantam, 1975.

*The Lathe of Heaven.* New York: Scribner's Sons, 1971; London: Gollancz, 1972; New York: Avon, 1972.

*The Left Hand of Darkness.* New York: Ace Books, 1969. London: Macdonald, 1969; New York: Harper & Row, 1980. Reprint. New York: Chelsea House, 1987.

*Malafrena.* New York: Putnam, 1979; London: Gollancz, 1980.

*Planet of Exile.* New York: Ace Books, 1966; London: Universal-Tandem, 1972; New York: Harper & Row, 1978.

*Rocannon's World.* (Bound with *The Kar-Chee Reign* by Avram Davidson.) New York: Ace Books, 1966; London: Universal Tandem, 1972; New York: Harper & Row, 1977.

*Tehanu: The Last Book of Earthsea.* New York: Atheneum, 1990.

*The Tombs of Atuan.* New York: Atheneum, 1970; London: Gollancz, 1972; New York: Bantam, 1975.

*Very Far Away from Anywhere Else.* New York: Atheneum, 1976; Published as *A Very Long Way from Anywhere Else,* London: Gollancz, 1976; New York: Bantam, 1978.

*Way of the Water's Going.* Texts from *Always Coming Home.* With photographers Ernest Waugh and Alan Nicholson. New York: Harper & Row, 1989.

*A Wizard of Earthsea.* Illustrated by Ruth Robbins. Berkeley: Parnassus/Houghton Mifflin, 1968; New York: Ace, 1970; Harmondsworth: Puffin, 1971; New York: Atheneum, 1991.

*The Word for World Is Forest.* New York: Putnam, 1976; New York: Berkley, 1976; London: Gollancz, 1977.

### Short Story Collections

*Buffalo Gals and Other Animal Presences.* Santa Barbara: Capra, 1987.

*Buffalo Gals, Won't You Come out Tonight.* Illustrations by Susan Seddon Boulet. San Francisco: Pomegranate Artbooks, 1994.

*The Compass Rose.* Underwood-Miller, 1982; New York: Harper & Row, 1982; New York: Bantam, 1983.

*A Fisherman of the Inland Sea.* New York: HarperPrism, 1994.

*Four Ways to Forgiveness.* New York: HarperPrism, 1995.

*The Ones Who Walk Away from Omelas.* New York: Creative Education, 1993. Previously published in *New Dimensions III,* ed. R. Silverberg. New York: Doubleday, 1973.

*Orsinian Tales.* New York: Harper & Row, 1976; New York: Bantam, 1983.

*Searoad: Chronicles of Klatsand.* New York: HarperCollins, 1991, 1992.

*Unlocking the Air.* New York: HarperCollins, 1996.

*The Wind's Twelve Quarters: Short Stories.* New York: Harper & Row, 1975; London, Gollancz, 1976; New York: Bantam, 1976.

### Books for Children

*Adventure in Kroy.* Illustrated by Alicia Austin. New Castle, VA: Cheap Street, 1982.

*The Adventures of Cobbler's Rune.* Illustrated by Alicia Austin. New Castle, VA: Cheap Street, 1982.

*Catwings.* Illustrated by S. D. Schindler. New York: Orchard Books, 1988.

*Catwings Return.* Illustrated by S. D. Schindler. New York: Orchard Books, 1989.

*Cobbler's Rune: Adventures in Kroy.* Illustrated by Alicia Austin. New Castle, VA: Cheap Street, 1983.

*Fire and Stone.* Illustrated by Laura Marshall. New York: Atheneum, 1989.

*Fish Soup.* Illustrated by Patrick Wynne. New York: Atheneum, 1992.

*Leese Webster.* Illustrated by James Brunsman. New York: Atheneum, 1979; London, Gollancz, 1981.

*A Ride on the Red Mare's Back.* Illustrated by Julie Downing. New Castle, VA: Cheap Street, 1992.

*Solomon Leviathan's Nine Hundred Thirty-First Trip Around the World.* Illustrated by Alicia Austin. Harmondsworth, England: Puffin, 1976; New Castle, VA: Cheap Street, 1983; New York: Philomel, 1988.

*A Visit from Dr. Katz.* Illustrated by Ann Barrow. New York: Atheneum, 1988.

*Wonderful Alexander and the Catwings.* Illustrations by S. D. Schindler. New York: Orchard Books, 1994.

### Poetry Collections

*Blue Moon over Thurman Street.* With photographer Roger Dorband. Portland, OR: NewSage, 1993.

*Going out with Peacocks and Other Poems.* New York: HarperCollins, 1994.

*Hard Words and Other Poems.* New York: Harper & Row, 1981.

*In the Red Zone.* With artist Henk Pander. Santa Barbara, CA: Lord John, 1983.

*Tillai and Tylissos.* With Theodora K. Quinn. San Francisco: Red Bull, 1979.

*Wild Angels.* Santa Barbara, CA: Capra, 1975.

*Wild Oats and Fireweed.* New York: Harper & Row, 1988.

### Drama

*King Dog.* Santa Barbara, CA: Capra, 1985.

### Essays and Lectures

*Dancing at the Edge of the World: Thoughts on Words, Women, Places.* New York: Grove, 1989; London: Gollancz, 1989.

*The Language of the Night: Essays on Fantasy and Science Fiction,* ed. Susan Wood. New York: Perigee, 1979. Revised ed. New York: HarperCollins, 1992.

### Anthologies Edited

*Edges: Thirteen New Tales from the Borderlands of the Imagination.* With Virginia Kidd. New York: Pocket Books, 1980.

*Interfaces: An Anthology of Speculative Fiction.* With Virginia Kidd. New York: Grosset & Dunlap/Ace, 1980.

*Nebula Award Stories XI.* New York: Harper & Row, 1977.

*The Norton Book of Science Fiction.* With Brian Attebery and Karen Fowler. New York: Norton, 1993.

### Audio Recordings

*The Earthsea Trilogy.* (Abridged.) London: Colophon, 1981.

*Gwilan's Harp* and *Intercom.* Read by UKL. New York: Caedmon, 1977.

*The Left Hand of Darkness.* (Abridged.) Read by UKL. New York: Warner Audio, 1985.

*Music and Poetry of the Kesh.* Text by UKL. Music by Todd Barton. Ashland, OR: Valley Productions, 1985.
*Rigel Nine: An Opera.* Libretto by UKL. Music by David Bedford. London: Charisma, 1985.

## Secondary Works

### Books

Bittner, James. *Approaches to the Fiction of Ursula K. Le Guin.* Ann Arbor, MI: UMI Research Press, 1984; Essex: Bowker, 1984.

Bloom, Harold, ed. *Modern Critical Views: Ursula K. Le Guin.* New York: Chelsea House, 1986.

Bloom, Harold, ed. *Modern Critical Interpretations: Ursula K. Le Guin's "The Left Hand of Darkness."* New York: Chelsea House, 1987.

Bucknall, Barbara J. *Ursula K. Le Guin.* New York: Frederick Ungar, 1981.

Cummins, Elizabeth. *Understanding Ursula K. Le Guin.* Columbia, SC: University of South Carolina, 1990.

De Bolt, Joe. *Ursula K. Le Guin: Voyager to Inner Lands and to Outer Space.* Port Washington, NY: Kennikat Press, 1979.

Keulen, Margarete. *Radical Imagination: Feminist Conceptions of the Future in Ursula K. Le Guin, Marge Piercy and Sally Miller Gearhart.* New York: Peter Lang, 1991.

Olander, Joseph, and Martin Greenberg, eds. *Ursula K. Le Guin.* New York: Taplinger, 1979.

Selinger, Bernard. *Le Guin and Identity in Contemporary Fiction.* Ann Arbor: University of Michigan Press, 1988.

Spivack, Charlotte. *Ursula K. Le Guin.* Boston: Twayne, 1984.

Slusser, George Edgar. *The Farthest Shores of Ursula K. Le Guin.* Popular Writers of Today: The Milford Series. San Bernardino, CA: Borgo, 1976.

### Articles

"Ursula K. Le Guin." In *Authors and Artists for Young Adults,* vol. 9. Detroit: Gale Research, 1992.

Barbour, Douglas. "The Lathe of Heaven: Taoist Dream." *Algol* 21 (November 1973): 22–24.

Baumann, Paul, "So Many Books, So Little Time." *Commonweal* 16, no. 14 (11 August 1989): 438–441.

Berkley, Miriam. "Ursula K. Le Guin." *Publishers Weekly* (23 May 1986): 72.

Bleiler, E. F. "Ursula K. Le Guin." In *Dictionary of Literary Biography.* New York: Scribners, 1985.

Clute, John. "Deconstructing Paradise." *Times Literary Supplement* (28 December 1990): 1409.

Commire, Ann, ed. "Ursula K. Le Guin." In *Something About the Author*. Detroit: Gale Research, 1987.

Dezell, Maureen. "Ursula K. Le Guin: Still Toying with Fantasy, Reality." *Boston Globe* (3 August 1994): 65.

Esmonde, Margaret. "The Master Pattern: The Psychological Journey in the Earthsea Trilogy." In Joseph Olander and Martin Greenberg, eds. *Ursula K. Le Guin* (New York: Taplinger, 1979): 15–35.

Fadiman, Anne. "Ursula K. Le Guin: Voyager to the Inner Land." *Life* 9, no. 4 (April 1986): 23–25.

Gordon, Andrew. "Ursula K. Le Guin." In *Dictionary of Literary Biography*. Detroit: Gale Research, 1986.

"A Hole in the World." *Times Literary Supplement* (6 April 1973): 3709.

Le Guin, Ursula K. "Children, Women, Men and Dragons." In *Earthsea Revisioned*. Cambridge: Green Bay, 1993.

Littlefield, Holly. "Unlearning Patriarchy: Ursula K. Le Guin's Feminist Consciousness in *The Tombs of Atuan* and *Tehanu*." *Extrapolation* (Fall 1995): 244–258.

Mandelbaum, Paul, ed. "Ursula K. Le Guin." In *First Words*. Chapel Hill, NC: Algonquin Books, 1993.

McKinley, Robin. "The Woman Wizard's Triumph," *New York Times Book Review* (12 May 1990): 38.

Prescott, Jani, and Jean Ross. "Ursula K. Le Guin," In *Contemporary Authors: New Revision Series*. Detroit: Gale Research, 1991.

Samuelson, David. "Ursula K. Le Guin." *Supernatural Fiction Writers*. New York: Scribners, 1985.

Shippey, T. A. "The Magic Art and the Evolution of Works: Ursula K. Le Guin's Earthsea Trilogy." *Mosaic* 10 (Winter 1977): 158.

"Ursula K. Le Guin Issue." *Science-Fiction Studies* (March 1976).

Votteler, Thomas, ed. "Ursula K. Le Guin." In *Contemporary Literary Criticism*. Detroit: Gale Research, 1992.

Walsh, William. "I Am a Woman Writer; I Am a Western Writer: an Interview with Ursula K. Le Guin." *Kenyon Review* (Summer 1995): 192–205.

Watson, Ian. "Le Guin's *Lathe of Heaven* and the Role of Dick: The False Reality as Mediator." *Science-Fiction Studies* 2 (March 1975): 67–75.

White, Jonathan. "Coming Back from the Silence." *Whole Earth Review* 85 (Spring 1995): 76–83.

## Bibliography

Cogell, Elizabeth Cummins. *Ursula K. Le Guin: A Primary and Secondary Bibliography*. Boston: G. K. Hall, 1983.

### Manuscript Collection

University of Oregon Library, Eugene, Oregon.

**Selected Book Reviews**

*Always Coming Home:*

Johnson, Brian. "Always Coming Home." *Maclean's Magazine* (4 November 1985): 72.
Kirchhoff, H. J. "Always Coming Home." *Toronto Globe & Mail* (7 December 1985): 195.

*Children's Books:*

Dragonwings, Crescent. "Upward Mobility in the Kitty Ghetto." *New York Times Book Review* (13 November 1988): 40.
Flowers, Ann. "Catwings." *The Horn Book* (March 1989): 206.
Iarusso, Marilyn. "Catwings Returns." *School Library Journal* (August 1989): 124.
Vandergrift, Kay. "A Ride on the Red Mare's Back." *School Library Journal* (September 1992): 207.
Wynne, Patrick. "Fish Soup." *School Library Journal* (January 1993): 80.

*Dancing at the Edge of the World:*

Perrin, Noel. "Father Tongue, Mother Tongue." *New York Times Book Review* (12 March 1989): 18.

*Earthsea Cycle:*

Dirda, Michael. "Tehanu." *Book World* (25 February 1990): 9.
"Earthsea Revisited." *Times Literary Supplement* (28 April 1972): 484.
LaFaille, Gene. "Science Fiction Universe." *Wilson Library Bulletin* (June 1990): 124.
"The Making of a Mage." *Times Literary Supplement* (2 April 1971): 383.
McKinley, Robin. "The Woman Wizard's Triumph." *New York Times Book Review* (20 May 1990): 38.
Neill, Heather. "Strong as Women's Magic—*Tehanu*," *Times Educational Supplement* (9 November 1990): R9.
O'Brien, Dennis. "Earthsea." *Commonweal* (9 December 1977): 25.
Tax, Meredith. "Fantasy Island." *Village Voice* (30 October 1990): 75.
Waits, Cara. "*Tehanu: The Last Book of Earthsea* by Ursula K. Le Guin." *Wilson Book Bulletin* (September 1991): 514.

*A Fisherman of the Inland Sea:*

Lerner, Fred. "Science Fiction Multiverse." *Wilson Library Supplement* (April 1995): 94.
Steinberg, Sybil. "*A Fisherman of the Inland Sea*." *Publishers Weekly* (28 November 1994): 47.

*Four Ways to Forgiveness:*

"*Four Ways to Forgiveness.*" *Publishers Weekly* (24 July 1995): 51.

*Poetry and Short Story Collections:*

Allen, Frank. "Going out with Peacocks and Other Poems." *Library Journal* (1 July 1994): 110.
O'Rourke, Rebecca. "Buffalo Gals and Other Animal Presences." *New Statesman & Society* (16 March 1990): 38.
Steinberg, Sybil. "Buffalo Gals and Other Animal Presences." *Publishers Weekly* (24 July 1987): 176.

*Searoad:*

Armstrong, Isobel. "Searoad." *Times Literary Supplement* (13 March 1992): 23.
Engel, Monroe. "Searoad." *New York Times Book Review* (12 January 1992): 10.

# Appendix

## Selected Honors and Awards

*A Wizard of Earthsea:* Boston Globe Horn Book Award for Excellence (1969).

*Tombs of Atuan:* Newbery Honor (Silver) (1972); National Book Award finalist (1972).

*The Farthest Shore:* National Book Award (1973).

*The Left Hand of Darkness:* Nebula (1969); Hugo (1970).

*The Dispossessed:* Hugo (1975); Jupiter (1975); Nebula (1975); Jules Verne Award (1975); American Library Association's Best Books for Young Adults List (1974).

*The Word for World Is Forest:* Hugo (1973); National Book Award finalist (1976).

*Very Far Away from Anywhere Else:* American Library Association's Best Books for Young Adult List (1976); Horn Book honor list (1976); Prix Lectures-Jeunesse (translation by Laroche) (1987).

*The Beginning Place:* American Library Association's Best Books for Young Adults list (1980).

*Always Coming Home:* Nominated for American Book Award (1985); Janet Heidinger Kafka Prize for Fiction (1986).

*Buffalo Gals and Other Animal Presences:* Hugo (1987); International Fantasy Award (1989).

*Tehanu: The Last Book of Earthsea:* Nebula (1990).

*Searoad:* Pushcart Prize for "Bill Weisler" (1991); Harold Vursell (1991); American Award & Institute of Arts and Letters (1991); H. L. Davis Award from Oregon Institute of Literary Arts (1992).

*Four Ways to Forgiveness: Asimov's* Readers' Award for "Forgiveness Day" (1995).

Selected Short Story Awards: "The Diary of the Rose": Jupiter (1976).

Selected Poetry Awards: Hubbub poetry award for "Semen" (1995).

117

# INDEX

119

# The Author

Suzanne Elizabeth Reid lives in the mountains of southwestern Virginia, where she teaches courses in English, Young Adult Literature, Western Tradition, and Education at Emory and Henry College. She has published articles about teaching and young adult literature in various journals, including the *ALAN Review* and *Signal,* and a previous book, *Presenting Cynthia Voigt.* When she is not teaching, reading, and writing, she likes to bike with her husband and talk (at length) with friends and her two children, Jenny and Tristan. In an attempt to return the lawn to land habitable by wildlife, she has replaced most of the grass with whatever will grow. Outside the window near her desk is a small pond, where two frogs, three fish, and an occasional snake reward her efforts.

# The Editor

Patricia J. Campbell is an author and critic specializing in books for young adults. She has taught adolescent literature at UCLA and is the former Assistant Coordinator of Young Adult Services for the Los Angeles Public Library. Her literary criticism has been published in the *New York Times Book Review* and many other journals. From 1978 to 1988 her column "The YA Perplex," a monthly review of young adult books, appeared in the *Wilson Library Bulletin*. She now writes a column on controversial issues in adolescent literature for *Horn Book* magazine. Campbell is the author of five books, among them *Presenting Robert Cormier*, the first volume in the Twayne Young Adult Author Series. In 1989 she was the recipient of the American Library Association Grolier Award for distinguished achievement with young people and books. A native of Los Angeles, Campbell now lives on an avocado ranch near San Diego, where she and her husband David Shore write and publish books on overseas motorhome travel.